Wonderful
ONE-PATCH
QUILTS

20 Projects from Triangles, Half-Hexagons, Diamonds & More

Sara Nephew and Marci Baker

C&T PUBLISHING

Text and photography copyright © 2017 by Sara Nephew and Marci Baker

Photography and artwork copyright © 2017 by C&T Publishing, Inc.

Publisher: Amy Marson

Creative Director: Gailen Runge

Editors: Lynn Koolish and Joanna Burgarino

Technical Editors: Debbie Rodgers and Gailen Runge

Cover Designer: April Mostek

Book Designer: Kristen Yenche

Production Coordinator: Zinnia Heinzmann

Production Editor: Alice Mace Nakanishi

Illustrator: Eric Sears

Photo Assistants: Carly Jean Marin and Mai Yong Vang

Instructional photography by Diane Pedersen of C&T Publishing, unless otherwise noted

Published by C&T Publishing, Inc., P.O. Box 1456, Lafayette, CA 94549

Library of Congress Cataloging-in-Publication Data
Names: Nephew, Sara, author. | Baker, Marci L., author.
Title: Wonderful one-patch quilts : 20 projects from triangles, half-hexagons, diamonds & more / Sara Nephew and Marci Baker.
Description: Lafayette, CA : C&T Publishing, Inc., [2017]
Identifiers: LCCN 2016030018 | ISBN 9781617454677 (soft cover)
Subjects: LCSH: Patchwork--Patterns. | Quilting--Patterns.
Classification: LCC TT835 .N4626 2017 | DDC 746.46--dc23
LC record available at https://lccn.loc.gov/2016030018

Printed in the USA

10 9 8 7 6 5 4 3 2 1

Dedication

To all my grandchildren:

Taylor, Ashley, Skye, Zev, Rykker, Griffin, and Hazel.
You seven are a whole new fun club to belong to.

·····*Sara*

To Mom and Dad:

Thank you for teaching me perseverance.

·····*Marci*

Acknowledgments

Thank you to all the quilters who made the beautiful quilts featured in this book:

Annette Austin · Janet Blazekovich · Joyce Lawrence Cambron
Diane Riley Coombs · Pam J. Cope · Scott Hansen
Deborah Haynes · Elaine Muzichuk · Sarah Ann Newman
Jeanne Rumans · Janice Schlieker · Kathy Syring
Linda Tellesbo · Susan Porretta Weigner
and to Martha Ethridge for testing the Reflections technique

Each creation provided added beauty to the projects, and we can't
thank you enough for your feedback on the instructions and your
trust that we would present your works in their best light.

Thank you to the companies that provided supplies for several of these projects:

Maywood Studio · Java Batiks · Moda Fabrics
Presencia Thread · Quilter's Dream Batting · YLI Corporation

Their support of the art and craft of quilting through manufacturing
superior products makes our job (and passion) even more enjoyable.

CONTENTS

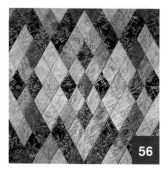

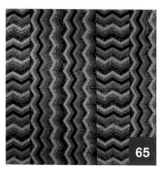
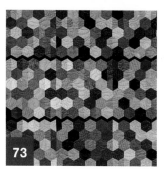

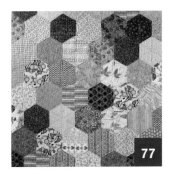
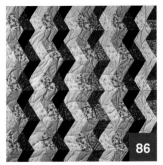

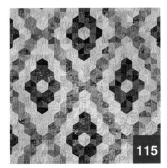
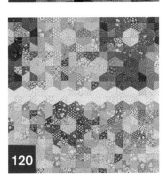

Beginning Again —○ *by Sara*

When I was a new quilter, I loved many quilts, but my favorites were those from the past. I'm sure these were the same favorites that many other quilters have, including classic patterns such as Trip Around the World, Grandmother's Flower Garden, and Thousand Pyramids. These patterns were simple, but the quilters used a mix of beautiful colors and special color arrangements to create designs that would please just about anyone.

Now, thirty years later, I have created many quilt designs of my own: floral-looking quilts, stacked repeats, three-dimensional designs…. Yet I still enjoy making patterns that are like those classic quilts I've always loved, in which the pieces used are simple but the pattern is special because of a great mix of colors and the arrangement of the colors and values.

Detail of *Rolling Ball* (page 38)

Nowadays we have many more tools and techniques to make quilting faster and easier. These new tools and techniques lead to new patterns being born. Sixty-degree rulers let us cut shapes that rarely before, if ever, would have been used in a quilt. These new shapes, in turn, inspire new patterns and combinations. With this innovation we have the opportunity to make new classics in the same vein as those simple vintage charmers, and I hope many quilters will want to make and enjoy them. That's what this book is about.

The patterns in this book are made from units that are easy enough even for beginners. Use the patterns to play with your fabrics by mixing colors and values as you make your quilts. In each project we provide guidance on color, value, and placement, which make all the difference in your quilt's success.

Skim through the book to see what the pattern testers have chosen for their colors and fabrics; then pick a pattern that you like and add sparkling high-contrast colors or a soft color-wash effect in *your* favorite colors to bring out the best in the pattern.

I hope to see your individualized quilt shining in a quilt show or online. Each person's choices of color, texture, pattern, and theme change the pattern into a new, special quilt. I'm looking forward to seeing all the new classic quilts these patterns inspire.

Tradition with a New Process ⟲ *by Marci*

Wow! That was all I could say when I first viewed the variety of designs that Sara put together for this book. Our collaboration gives us unique opportunities to demonstrate where our particular talents lie. Sara's eye for design shows in a pattern's underlying structure ("the bones," as she puts it, created by value contrast) and color scheme (the colors, tones, and clarity, which give feeling or emotion to that underlying structure). My talents, and heart, resonate with figuring out the most efficient and effective ways to craft her designs. (Okay, it is probably my brain more than it is my heart!)

Some quilters hear the words *speed piecing, strip piecing,* or *fast method* and think the process involves slashing through fabric, slapping pieces together, and getting on to the next quilt without any care for quality. That is far from my intent! The process of working with fabrics, making selections, cutting shapes, sewing small pieces or strips to be cut later, arranging pieces for the blocks, and, finally, joining the last pieces of the top are all part of the joy of quilting. The techniques I have developed are intended to give value to those steps by adding an ease and precision that can surprise even the newest quilter. My hope is that because of my techniques, quilters will explore even more quilt designs and methods.

There are times, however, when a faster method does not work, such as with charm quilts. These unique quilts, in which each piece is from a different fabric, are only achievable when the pieces are cut individually. There is a meditative quality to this type of quilt. I have made a couple of these quilts already—my first quilt and my most challenging quilt. For this book I started another such quilt: *Grand Hex* (page 94). Thus the techniques in this book have been selected to provide a more traditional piecing method as well as a speed-piecing method. Select the method that fits your style. Or try the other method and see if it suits you. You might be surprised!

Barbie Doll **by Marci Baker**
Photo by Randy Pfizenmaier

Building on the Years **by Marci Baker**
Photo by Randy Pfizenmaier

I hope that you find several new classics among Sara's designs in this book, and that you enjoy the underlying methods incorporated by both of us.

INTRODUCTION

What Is a Classic?

Part of our reason for writing this book is to create new designs that we hope will become classics. People talk about classic cars, classic clothes, and classic quilts. So … what is a classic? The biggest element of any classic is its design. If the object is beautiful to look at, so much so that lots of people have decided to have one, it's possibly a classic. If it holds up well over time, it's definitely a classic. If it was fun to look at 50 years ago and it is fun to look at now, it's classic.

Most quilt patterns are based on a mathematical grid. This grid is easy to see with pieced quilts. Appliqué quilts, too, should have a strong underlying structure, but many people will not able to tell what that structure is. A good underlying structure, the grid, is what gives quilts a strong and appealing design.

Most quilters are very familiar with designs based on a 90° grid; this grid uses squares and half-squares.

Many of these designs are classics, including the Nine-Patch, Postage Stamp, Trip Around the World, and Irish Chain patterns. Templates for any quilt pattern using this grid can be created by folding a piece of paper or drawing on graph paper.

We, however, really like designs based on a 60° grid. Shapes created by using these angles are strong and easy to piece. With a 60° grid, you can make fun designs that have never been made before!

Some classic designs are already based on the 60° grid. Grandmother's Flower Garden and Thousand Pyramids are two such familiar patterns. With the new tools now available to quilters, you can create even more patterns that take advantage of this set of shapes, are easy to piece, and are very appealing in style. Classic quilts indeed!

Perhaps, with inspiration from the patterns in this book, you can create a quilt that is a new classic!

About These Projects

The approach taken to all the patterns in this book is as simple as possible, in order to make the pieces easy to handle and straightforward to sew. All the patterns are based on the 60° angle, which creates our favorite shapes. For the sake of simplicity, we concentrate on just one shape in each quilt. Projects are divided into sections based on which shape is featured in the design. There are sections for triangle halves, triangles, diamonds and long diamonds, half-hexagons (also known as *trapezoids*), and quarter-hexagons.

Quarter-hexagon in *Diamond Path* (page 111)

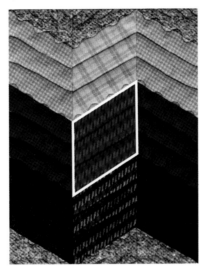

Triangle halves in *Crystal Night* (page 29)

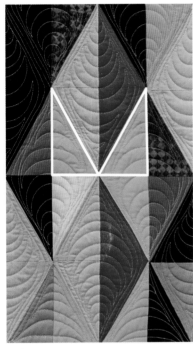

Triangles in *Fantasy* (page 46)

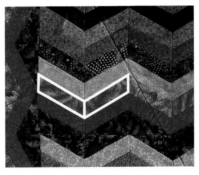

Diamonds (red check) in *Don't Tread on Me* (page 61)

Long diamond in *Country Road* (page 65)

Half-hexagon in *Bubbles* (page 77)

Sometimes the edge of the block, the edge of the quilt, or a corner will cut up the shapes. All these projects use fill-in pieces that are part of the featured piece in order to make a straight edge on the block or quilt. Similarly, we found ways to avoid having set-in pieces, which often are not fun to piece.

The projects are rotary cut and machine pieced; you can, however, use scissors and hand piecing if you prefer (see Patterns, page 124). Directions for rotary cutting the shapes are in given in each section:

Triangle Halves (page 23)

Triangles (page 32)

Diamonds and Long Diamonds (page 50)

Half-Hexagons (page 70)

Quarter-Hexagons (page 91)

Follow your color and fabric inspirations, prepare your fabric, and start cutting shapes to create a unique one-patch quilt that everyone will love.

Piecing Blocks versus Strip Piecing

Blocks: Sara's Process ∘─ *by Sara*

Sara prefers to work with blocks; she finds them easier to handle because they have a limited number of pieces. For example, for Thousand Pyramids, she thinks a triangular block is easier to handle than rows of many triangles sewn together. That block became her contribution toward a *new* classic quilt based on Thousand Pyramids.

Detail of Thousand Pyramids block (page 33)

In many of these designs, the block is quite large. You can use just one block as a wallhanging or baby quilt or combine as many blocks as needed for your desired quilt size.

Strips: Marci's Process ∘─ *by Marci*

Marci prefers to work with strip-cutting and strip-piecing methods, which quite often involve sewing together long pieced strips. In so doing she trades the possibility of truly scrappy or charm quilts for planned projects with fewer fabrics. Many of her quilts can still *look* scrappy, but not as much as quilts made using Sara's method. For example, in *Fantasy* (page 46), pairs of triangles are cut from strips that were previously sewn together. Then those pairs are sewn into rows across the block. Because the same two fabrics are sewn together first, they always appear in the same pattern order, which fits this quilt's radiating design.

Full row of triangles from *Fantasy* (page 46)

Another trade-off in Marci's process is that you usually will be working with the bias edges of the fabric. If this is a challenge for you, see Tip: Working with Bias (page 31).

FABRICS

Fiber Content

Usually quilters achieve the best results using 100% cotton quilting-weight fabric from a quilt store. Quilters have also traditionally used scraps left over from making clothes, pieces cut from used clothing (although these pieces might not hold up well), or various specialty fabrics, such as blends, silks, satins, or decorator fabrics. If you choose to not buy fabric, you can use scraps for the projects in this book, but do try to use good quality scraps that will best showcase your work.

COTTON—THE BEST FABRIC

Most quilts are made from cotton fabric. We recommend 100% cotton quilting-weight fabric, and that is what most of our personal quilts are made from. Pure cotton quilting-weight fabric is flexible, soft, and easy to both handle and care for. It will wear well, especially if you wash it by hand, and only when necessary.

FLANNEL

Flannel is a worthwhile fabric to use in a quilt. As a gift for someone who loves a warm and fuzzy feeling, a flannel quilt is tops. Some flannels are pretty tight and substantial, while others seem a little more loosely woven. Either way, flannel tends to shrink. Therefore be sure to prewash your flannel fabric. If you take your time learning to use it, flannel will make wonderful quilts. Some of the projects in this book use larger pieces that are perfect for flannel.

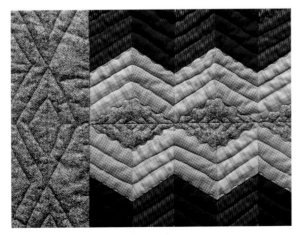

Detail of *Don't Tread on Me* (page 61)

DECORATOR FABRIC

The designs of decorator fabrics can be quite different than those of quilt-shop fabrics. The projects in this book that use larger pieces are good candidates for decorator fabrics with large-scale patterns. Generally decorator fabrics tend to be thicker and more expensive than quilt-shop fabrics.

For an easy source of decorator fabrics, try visiting an upholstery shop to ask if they have any sample books they intend to throw away. You can take these sample books home, pry them apart, and use the pieces of fabric.

Detail of *Meteorite* (page 42)

SPECIALTY FABRIC

Silks and satins add sparkle and shine you can't get in any other way, so many quilters like to try them. These fabrics can be challenging because they are slippery and tend to ravel. There are many methods for dealing with slippery fabrics, such as stabilizing shifting fabric with lightweight fusible interfacing. Each quilter who works with specialty fabrics has a preferred method for working with them. Find your preferred method. Or you might want to just pass on these fabrics for now.

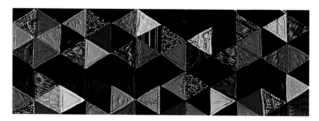

Detail of *Antique Thousand Pyramids*; collection of Marci Baker

Fabric Effects

THE SCRAPPY LOOK

Many quilters enjoy the "scrappy look" created when many different fabrics are used in one quilt; because of this, several projects in this book are "scrappy." This look is surprisingly traditional because many vintage quilts were pieced from leftover scraps of sewing fabric or pieces given to quilters by others. To this day, some quilters still trade scraps.

With the scrappy look, the goal is to use lots of scraps—and thus lots of fabrics. Using a large quantity of different fabrics that vary in value, scale, and color adds richness and interest to the final quilt.

Detail of *Watercolor Garden* (page 103)

VALUE

Pay attention to the color, value, and texture of all the fabrics you are using as you make the blocks. Evaluate what you have put together for color value. How light, medium, or dark are the fabrics compared with each other? Do they provide strong lines, or do the lines fade together? For a multiblock project, is your first block bold and high contrast? Apart from its value contrast, do you like the color combination? You can soften the contrast or add a different color combination in the next block if you decide to try something different. As you keep constructing and adding blocks, think of yourself as a juggler, keeping all the balls in the air by keeping the balance and action going. Stay sensitive to the result of each additional block to achieve a lovely quilt.

Detail of *Fancy Flowers* (page 120)

SCALE

You also need to be in control of the scale of the fabrics you are combining. A mix of print design sizes is visually interesting, whereas fabrics with print designs all the same scale may end up looking boring or too coherent, such that the effect is flat and detracts from the overall quilt design.

THEME

Finally, judge whether the fabric themes fit together. Soft floral prints of various sizes and colors make a great watercolor-type quilt. But adding a cartoonlike polar-bear print, for example, may produce a jarring touch in the design. You are the artist, the fabric painter, and you will learn what you like and what you do not like while creating your own great quilts.

Detail of *Grand Hex Variation* (page 98)

To Wash or Not to Wash

That is the question.

Most quilters have their own preferences for prewashing. Some follow the process they first learned when they started quilting. Through experience each of us has found our favorite way to handle the fabric, and we share our preferences below.

Wash Fabric ◦—*by Sara*

I wash my fabric *by hand* for two reasons. First, you can see if any colors are running and use one of the clever cures for this problem that you can learn at quilt shops or classes. Second, handwashing (or wetting) takes out less of the fabric's finish, leaving it crisp and with a good hand. Machine washing takes away more of the finish, making the fabric limp, potentially gauzy, and prone to raveling.

Don't Wash Fabric ◦—*by Marci*

Early in my quilting life, I was taught to wash my fabrics first. On my first few projects, I went immediately to cutting, and then, remembered I was supposed to have prewashed my fabric. I told myself, "Next time I'll do that." But that next time never arrived, because I like the crispness of an unwashed fabric's finish and because it takes me less time to complete a project if I don't prewash.

I use Shout Color Catcher sheets when I do finally wash the quilt. They help me determine if the quilt needs to have a second or third washing to remove the majority of excess dye.

Even when washing the fabric before cutting, I recommend using Color Catcher sheets. Washing a fabric once does not guarantee that all the excess dye is out, and you don't want the dye to run after it is pieced into the quilt.

THE BEST TOOLS FOR FAST METHODS

For the projects in this book, you can easily cut one piece at a time with scissors or a rotary cutter, and it can be fun to use up scraps that way. It takes a little longer, but the process can be like meditation. This process allows for charm quilts or incorporation of a variety of fabrics.

Of course, a rotary cutter and mat speed up cutting a lot. Clever planners can now sew, stack, and cut strips, all with the goal of finishing a quilt top sooner rather than later. These speedy methods (and some new ones that we have developed) are used in this book for one reason in particular: The faster you go, the more quilts you can make. And we hope to inspire you to make more!

Tools

The tools needed to rotary cut these patterns are very basic. We list our favorite brands in parentheses following each item.

- **Rotary cutter** (Olfa): The 45 mm is the best size for speed and safety.

- **Self-healing mat** (Olfa)

- **6″ × 12″ ruler** (Omnigrid or Creative Grid): To see how we cut strips with this ruler and *never* get a crooked strip, see Cutting Strips (page 16).

- **60° ruler** (Clearview Triangle 60° Acrylic Ruler, size 8″ or 10″, or Clearview Triangle Super 60 Acrylic Ruler, both from C&T Publishing): *Note: We will refer to these throughout the book as the Clearview Triangle and Clearview Super 60 ruler.*

- **Corner-trimming tool** (Corner Cut 60—2-in-1 Sewing Tool, from C&T Publishing): Trimming the points for accurate and efficient piecing.

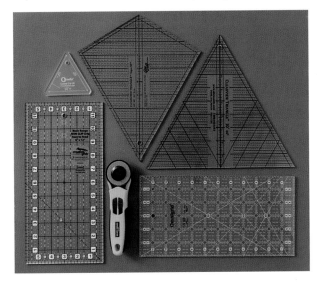

CAUTION!

If you choose to use another manufacturer's 60° ruler, be sure to check your work as you go. The projects in this book were designed for the Clearview Triangle or Clearview Super 60 ruler, so we highly recommend you use those. Other rulers, especially those with the tip flattened, can measure differently than what is illustrated here. (Clearview Triangle and Clearview Super 60 rulers are available from C&T Publishing.)

Methods and Tools Together

All the shapes used in these quilt projects are cut based on a strip of fabric and the Clearview Triangle or Clearview Super 60 ruler. The top point is a 60° angle, and the center line of the ruler has inch marks measured from the top. Nothing in this book is difficult to do if you focus on the relationship of the ruler to the strip. Even working with only these two elements, you can cut many shapes in whatever sizes you desire.

In fact, one of the reasons Sara developed the Clearview Triangle ruler was to have so many options. With it, you don't need a template for every size and shape—you just need one ruler!

Cutting Strips

This method allows fabric strips to be cut easily and successfully without turning around the mat or uncut fabric after squaring up. Even more importantly, it lets you know that the strips will be straight before cutting.

1. Fold your fabric selvage to selvage, sliding the selvages left or right until they are parallel and there are no wrinkles in the fabric. Press or smooth out the layers.

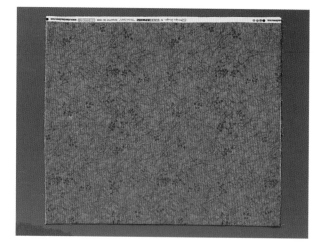

2. Fold the fabric again with the first fold pulled up just over the selvage.

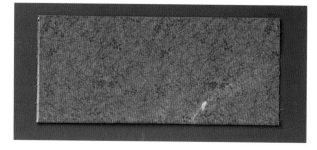

3. From the *left end* of the fabric, use the 6″ × 12″ ruler to measure that the folds are parallel. If they are not parallel, one side of fabric will be longer than the other. To fix this, lift and move the top single-fold slightly toward the end that is longer. Measure again and adjust until both folds are parallel.

4. At the left end of the fabric, align the ruler so that it is parallel to the top and bottom folds and covers the strip width (plus any leftover fabric, which we like to call the "scrap"). Cut on the right-hand side of the ruler.

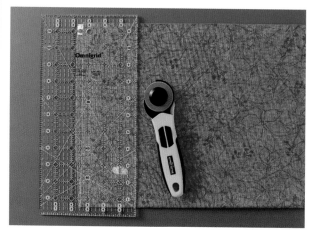

5. Turn the small cut piece 180°. Align the ruler with the top and bottom folds, with the cut width along the left edge. Trim off the scrap at the right-hand side of the ruler.

······ *tip* ······

C IS FOR *CUT*

Because this is different than how most of our students cut, we teach them this hint to remember: "C is for cut—Look for the C when aligning the ruler." The C is the part of the ruler that extends past the parallel folds and the cut edge of the fabric. If there is not a C, then it is time to realign the fabric so that the folds are parallel.

6. Continue aligning the ruler with the folds and straight edge and cutting strips from the remaining fabric until you have the required number of strips. If the top fold, the edge measurement, and the bottom fold do not all line up, repeat Steps 3–5 to refold and trim the fabric to be square.

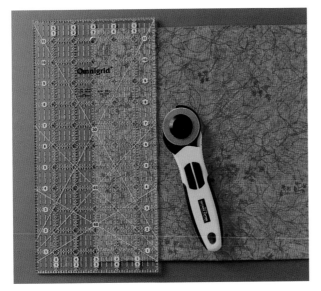

Aligning Triangles

FASTER ALIGNMENT WHEN SEWING ○─ *by Marci*

One challenge when working with triangles is that they need to be positioned properly for the seam allowance, which creates dog-ears. The places where the dog-ears stick out is where the seam needs to be. If the seam allowance does not hit those two points exactly, the pieces will become staggered, or crooked, in relation to each other.

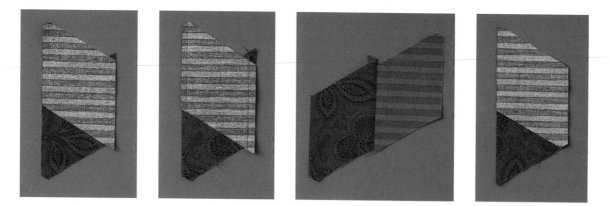

The solution is to either take your time while sewing to position the dog-ears so that they match the seam allowance or to trim off the dog-ears before sewing so that the pieces align quickly. Both solutions have their advantages, and it is your choice to make.

Sara leaves the dog-ears on because she is very familiar with her seam allowance and machine. She uses the dog-ears to align different portions of the piecing later in the sewing process. Moreover, trimming them off takes time, which she prefers to spend in other ways.

I have worked with the dog-ears on for many years because I, too, am comfortable with the seam allowance. I understand dog-ears well enough to work with anyone's seam allowance (for example, when teaching a class) and make the pieces match. Trimming the dog-ears off can take considerable time, and I have not found any quilting fairies to trim them for me!

However, I finally figured out, that to save significant time later at the sewing machine, I can take a little extra time when cutting the shapes. Before I even remove the pieces from the cutting mat, I now trim the dog-ears off. The time spent at the cutting mat is so much less than the time I used to spend aligning each seam at the machine. This method is also less frustrating because the pieces fit better and more consistently, and therefore their fit does not create issues down the road.

Throughout the instructions for cutting shapes in these projects, there are diagrams showing what dog-ears to trim. This task is done with the Corner Cut 60—2-in-1 Sewing Tool because it allows trimming for any 60° angle. Most, if not all, other rulers are designed for 45° angles. Also, the Corner Cut 60 tool marks where to trim for ¼", scant ¼", and generous ¼" seam allowances. These options make allowances for your variances in sewing, helping you get pieces that will always align and be straight when sewn.

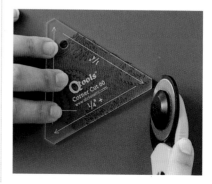

Pressing

TO ONE SIDE OR OPEN?

Traditionally seams are pressed to one side for quilting and pressed open for garment sewing. There are advantages to pressing a particular way for each type of project. Knowing the basics can give you the information you need to make decisions about when to use each method.

Pressed Open

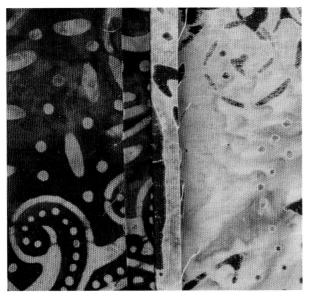

- Pressed-open seams are flatter and smoother, which is important on a three-dimensional figure.

- Pressed-open seams are easier to manipulate around curves—an important factor when constructing garments.

- Pressed-open seams do not create multiple layers of fabric in one area, and therefore the seams do not need to be graded. (Grading is a process whereby layers are trimmed to different widths to present a smoother transition rather than an abrupt edge.)

- Pressed-open seams produce a flatter look that can be attractive in certain quilted projects, especially wallhangings.

The task of pressing seams open can be quite challenging. There are methods that require pulling the fabric to make the seam open (essentially stretching the fabric), using your fingers or tools to manipulate the fabric directly in front of the iron, or working with a special narrow pressing stick that pushes the seam open.

Pressed to One Side

- Seams pressed to one side are stronger because the fabrics are in the same plane and cannot easily be pulled away from each other; this is especially true after quilting, when the quilting stitches hold them in place.

- Seams pressed to one side make matching points easy, because you can nest the seams together by having one seam pressed to the left and the other seam pressed to the right. (This is also called abutting seams, marrying seams, and opposing seams.) Minimal pinning is required, and the finished seams look great.

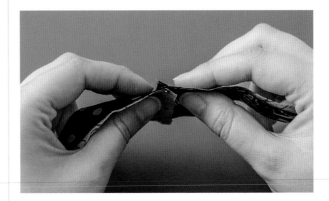

Pressing seams to one side can be done easily and successfully. Marci's favorite method is to cover her ironing board with flannel, which keeps the fabric from stretching even when using steam on straight or bias edges and gives a crisp press with no tucks or folds. Be sure to use a good iron and keep your hands away from the hot iron.

AN EXPERIMENT

Being the engineer that she is, Marci conducted an experiment to study, compare, and test the two types of pressing. She made a project in which half of the seams were pressed open and the other half were pressed to one side. She used the same stitch length, thread, and amount of quilting on both halves. After stretching and stressing the finished project, she found that some seams were fine but others had stitches that ripped.

Seams on the straight grain were fine for either pressing method. Basically, the seam's stitches were longer than the fabric could stretch.

Seams on the bias grain were broken for both pressing methods. Marci concluded that this was because the seam's stitches were shorter than the fabric could stretch when it was cut on the bias.

There were more places with ripped stitches on the seams that had been pressed open. This was because the two fabrics were pulling directly away from each other when the project was stretched. The holes were also more apparent than any that appeared in the seams pressed to one side, and these holes tended to become larger as the quilt was tugged on. (The holes in the seams pressed to one side did not grow larger.) The batting was visible, too.

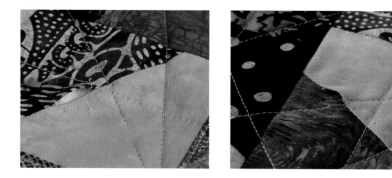

If a finished quilt has holes, it will be beneficial to repair them. To repair a pressed-open seam, use a ladder stitch that brings both sides together. This is not the easiest thing to do because getting your needle in the crease of each side so that the stitch does not show can be tricky. To repair a hole in a seam pressed to one side, use a common appliqué stitch that can be easily hidden, like the one used for sewing down binding. There are other ways to repair a ripped seam, but those are the two that we find best maintain the integrity and look of the original quilt.

RESOLUTION—OUR PRESSING PREFERENCE

Since Marci's experiment proved that both types of pressed seams can break when fabric pieces are cut on the bias, quilters need ways to mitigate this problem. One option is add sufficient quilting for the amount of use the quilt will get (keeping in mind the bias seams and their locations). Another is to shorten your stitch length, giving you a stitch more likely to handle the stress and stretch. This option, however, will take more time, use more thread, and make it more challenging to rip a seam should you make a mistake. A third option is to sew only projects with straight-grain pieces. This is not an option for most quilters, as there are too many intriguing designs that go beyond square corners!

Both of us have been making 60° quilts for decades, and—even with more than half of our seams being on the bias—broken seams have not been an issue. (In fact, the only quilt with broken-seam problems was one that Marci made with her son Kevin. It was tied rather than machine quilted, which caused the trouble.) We press our seams to one side, use a 2.5mm stitch length, and make sure to use sufficient machine quilting. If we do have any ripped stitches in our seams, they are not visible in the finished quilt because all seams are pressed to one side.

Because there are so many benefits and so few drawbacks, we prefer to press our seams to one side. Nevertheless, knowing the advantages of using a pressed-open seam in some circumstances gives us options when we need them.

Binding

BEST STRIP WIDTH ○—*by Marci*

Over the years I have changed the strip width that I use for binding. In the beginning it was based on whatever the pattern said to use. As I gained more experience and started comparing my bindings to see which looked good and which not so good, I learned what causes some common problems and how to modify my strip width to fix them.

A Couple of Issues

When judging quilt shows, the most common issue I see is rounded corners on binding. This is generally caused by using a binding strip that is too wide and then expecting the fold in the binding to fall directly on top of the stitching line. When the mitered corner is made for a ¼″ seam allowance on the front but there is extra fabric pushing to the front, the corners round out. One solution is to let the extra fabric fall to the back. There will be a wider binding on the back than on the front, but both sides will miter nicely, without a rounded corner. A second solution is to change the strip width as described at right.

Another issue with bindings is that the batting does not go all the way to the fold of the binding. This problem is also caused by a binding strip that is too wide. It is important to use the right size binding to fit your quilt, your seam allowance, and your batting (yes, that plays a part, too). Luckily, it is easy to figure this size so that you can get a great-looking binding without depending on a pattern (or other source) that is not customized to the details of your project.

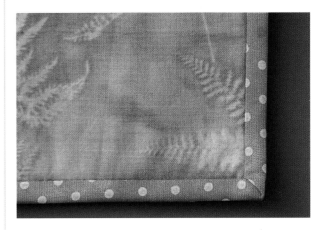

Figure *Your* Binding Width

The binding I use is called a *double-fold binding* or *French binding*. A strip is cut (either on the bias or the straight grain), folded in half, and applied to one side of the quilt with a seam allowance. Then, the strip is rolled to the other side of the quilt, where it is stitched down, either by hand or machine. This type of binding is easy to apply because the fold falls in place easily, and its two layers make it very durable. This cross section of the binding shows the different measurements to consider.

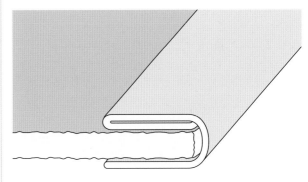

The questions to answer are:

1. How wide is your seam allowance, really?

Many quilters use a wider seam allowance when applying the binding than they do when piecing. This seam allowance can be measured from the edge of the quilt top or from the edge of the batting and backing if they are trimmed beyond the top.

2. What is the finished binding width on the front?

For these projects, make the finished width on the front the same as the seam allowance.

3. What is the thickness of your batting?

Most battings today are either ⅛″ or ¼″ thick. There are a few that are thicker or thinner. To measure, hold a ruler against an edge of the batting and, without squeezing the batting, read the thickness. (*Note: It is not critical enough to get into* ¹⁄₁₆″ *measurements.*)

4. What is the finished binding width on the back?

For your binding to be the same width on the front and back, the answer should match your answer to Question 2. I have heard that judges in some quilt shows take off points if your binding is not the same width on the front and back. I usually don't make my quilts for judges, so quite often I use different widths on the front and back so that it is easy to finish the binding by machine. (A judge probably would not like that either.) If you do not want to match the fold exactly with the stitch line, make this ⅛″ wider than the front width. Speaking from personal experience, I find that it is freeing to not have to sew right to the stitch line, especially if the seam wavered a little bit.

Now add up your answers to Questions 1–4 and multiply the total by 2.

Here are some examples:

Many quilters use a common ¼″ seam allowance and binding width on the front and back with ¼″ batting, so they answer ¼″ for each of these questions. These answers add up to 1″, which, when multiplied by 2, means using a 2″-wide binding strip. I also know many quilters who work with 2¼″- or 2½″-wide strips. If they think they are making the standard ¼″ binding, then they will have excess fabric to wrap to the back of the quilt.

For a ⅜″ binding on the front and back, with a ⅜″ seam allowance and ⅛″ batting, the figures add up to 1¼″, which, when multiplied by 2, equals 2½″. So if someone is cutting 2½″ binding strips, they need to be working with ⅜″ seam allowances.

One of my favorite bindings is a ¼″ binding on the front and back, with a ¼″ seam allowance and ⅛″ batting. When the numbers are added and multiplied by 2, the result is 1¾″-wide binding strips. These seem like such skinny strips, but on the right project, they make a definitive finish.

A Quick Reference

Here is a table that you can use to select your binding-strip width. With the information given here, you can also figure a different one that fits your project perfectly.

Binding Strip Width

Front and back binding width; seam allowance	Batting thickness		
	Low loft (⅛″)	Mid loft (¼″)	High loft (⅜″)
¼″	1¾″	2″	2¼″
⅜″	2½″	2¾″	3″

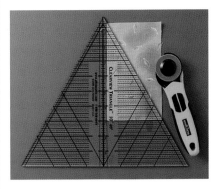

TRIANGLE HALVES

These instructions use the Clearview Triangle or Clearview Super 60 ruler (see Tools, page 14). If you choose to work with patterns instead, see Patterns (page 124).

Cut Triangle Halves

LEFT HALVES

Use a rectangle cut to the appropriate size. (For this example we used 3¾″ × 6½″.) Place the rectangle so that the shorter sides are horizontal. Place the ruler, point up, at the upper left corner and align the center line to the left edge of the rectangle. Cut along the right edge of the ruler. Trim off dog-ears, if desired, for faster sewing.

RIGHT HALVES

Use a rectangle cut to the appropriate size. (For this example we used 3¾″ × 6½″.) Arrange the rectangle and ruler as described in Left Halves (above), but this time have the ruler point down at the lower left corner. Cut along the right edge of the ruler. Trim off dog-ears, if desired, for faster sewing.

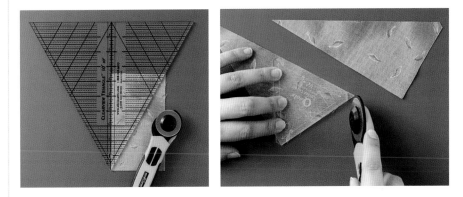

Speed Piece Triangle Halves into Half-Triangles

> ## note
>
> *The terms* triangle halves *and* half-triangles *might seem interchangeable at first, but they refer to two very different shapes.*
>
> **Triangle halves:** *These triangles are made by cutting a rectangle on the diagonal.*
>
> **Half-triangles:** *These triangles are made from two triangle halves.*

When there is repetition in the design, you can speed piece the triangle halves.

1. Use 2 rectangles cut to the appropriate size for your project. The project will also indicate the combinations to sew. With right sides together, sew these rectangles down both long sides.

2. Cut the rectangles, as described in Cut Triangle Halves (page 23), into left or right triangle halves, based on the project's instructions.

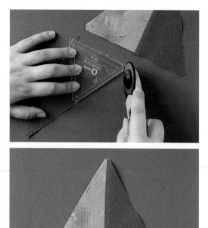

Speed Piece Triangle Halves into Long Half-Triangles

A second option is to speed piece the triangle halves by sewing on the shorter sides.

1. Use 2 rectangles cut to the appropriate size for your project. The project will also indicate the combinations to sew. With right sides together, sew these rectangles down both short sides.

3. Trim the dog-ears. Press the half-triangles as indicated in the project.

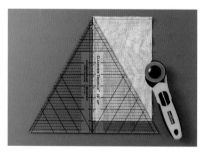

2. Cut the rectangles as described in Cut Triangle Halves (page 23) into left or right triangle halves, based on the project's instructions.

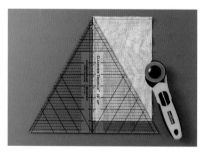

3. Trim the dog-ears. Press the long half-triangles as indicated in the project.

Sails

Made by Sara Nephew, quilted by Pam J. Cope

▲ **Finished block:** 6″ × 10½″ ▲ **Finished quilt:** 63″ × 72″

This quilt started with a blue batik fabric that had a checkered look. It ended, however, with a full assortment of solids—all combining to create sunshine, sky, red sails, the color of mountains, and so on. Like a Thousand Pyramids quilt, this quilt has triangle halves that build the illusion of larger shapes because of the color-value placement. The checkered border echoes the look of the original batik fabric.

YARDAGE

Light to light-medium: ¼ yard of at least 11 fabrics **or** 11 or more fat quarters

Medium-dark to dark: ¼ yard of at least 11 fabrics **or** 11 or more fat quarters

Border: 1¼ yards

Binding: ¾ yard

Backing: 4½ yards

Batting: 71″ × 80″

CUTTING

Light to light-medium

- Cut a total of 11 strips 6½″ × width of fabric. If using fat quarters, cut 22 strips 6½″ × 20″.

  From these strips, cut 108 rectangles 3¾″ × 6½″.

Medium-dark to dark

- Cut a total of 11 strips 6½″ × width of fabric. If using fat quarters, cut 22 strips 6½″ × 20″.

  From these strips, cut 108 rectangles 3¾″ × 6½″. Subcut 108 left and 108 right triangle halves. (Refer to Cut Triangle Halves, page 23, as needed.)

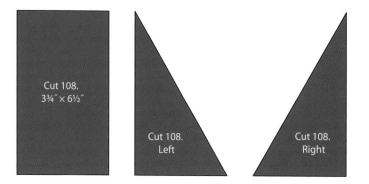

Border

- Cut 7 strips 5″ × width of fabric.

Binding

- Calculate the size needed for your style of binding (see Figure *Your* Binding Width, page 21). Cut 8 width-of-fabric strips in that size.

CONSTRUCTION

Seam allowances are ¼" unless otherwise noted.

Piece the Blocks

Follow the arrows for pressing direction.

Make the Half-Block

Refer to Speed Piece Triangle Halves into Half-Triangles (page 24) as needed.

1. Sew the light to light-medium rectangles in pairs down both lengthwise sides. Cut 108 half-triangles.

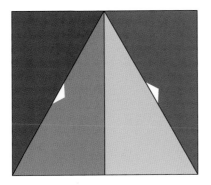

2. Sew the medium-dark to dark triangle halves to the 2 corners of the half-triangles. This half-block should measure 6½" × 5¾".

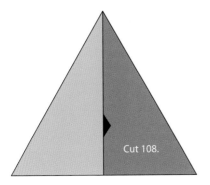

Make the Full Block

Pair the half-blocks to create the sails. Sew the pairs to make 54 blocks 6½" × 11". To reduce the bulk where the 4 pieces come together in the center, unstitch the last few stitches of the center vertical seams that are within the horizontal seam allowance, and press the horizontal seam half up and half down. This will allow the center seam to spin and be flat.

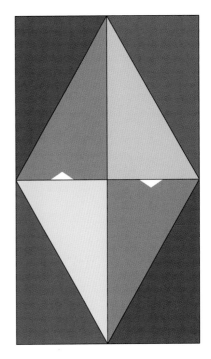

Piece the Quilt

1. Lay out the blocks to create a pleasing arrangement of values and colors. To reduce the size of the pieces to handle, sew the blocks into 9 sections. Sew these sections together into the finished quilt top.

2. Add the borders.

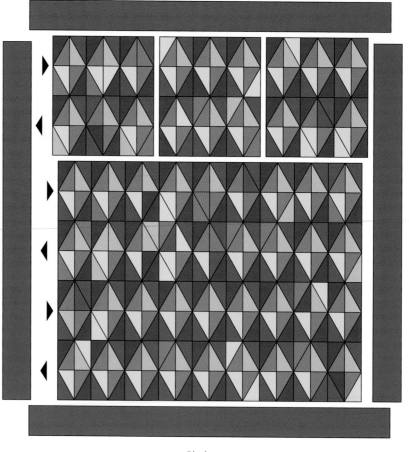

Piecing

Finish the Quilt

Layer, quilt, and bind to complete your quilt. Here is one suggestion for quilting that avoids the seam intersections.

Quilting

Crystal Night

Made by Janet Blazekovich

⬏ Finished quilt: 53″ × 70″

The fabric in this little quilt makes it sparkle like a crystal. The pattern uses the same basic block as the Sails quilt, but every other column of blocks has a half-block added at the top and bottom. This offsets the blocks and creates the zigzag effect. To make the process quicker, the pattern uses pre-sewn pieces that are assembled in rows rather than blocks. What fabrics and colors would you choose to make the crystal sparkle?

YARDAGE

Light to light-medium (kite shapes): ⅜ yard of 6 or more fabrics **or** 14 or more fat quarters (for a scrappier look)

Medium-dark to dark (zigzags): ⅜ yard of 6 or more fabrics **or** 14 or more fat quarters (for a scrappier look)

Border: 1 yard

Binding: ⅝ yard

Backing: 3½ yards

Batting: 61″ × 78″

CUTTING

Light to light-medium

* Cut a total of 6 strips 9″ × width of fabric. If using fat quarters, cut 14 strips 9″ × 20″.

  Subcut into 40 rectangles 5¼″ × 9″.

Medium-dark to dark

* Cut a total of 6 strips 9″ × width of fabric. If using fat quarters, cut 14 strips 9″ × 20″.

  Subcut into 40 rectangles 5¼″ × 9″.

Border

* Cut 6 strips 4½″ × width of fabric.

Binding

* Calculate the size needed for your style of binding (see Figure *Your* Binding Width, page 21). Cut 7 width-of-fabric strips in that size.

CONSTRUCTION

Seam allowances are ¼″ unless otherwise noted.

Piece the Long Half-Triangles

Follow the arrows for pressing direction.

1. Using pairs of light rectangles, make long half-triangles, following the directions in Speed Piece Triangle Halves into Long Half-Triangles (page 24). Press seams to the left. Make 40 light long half-triangles.

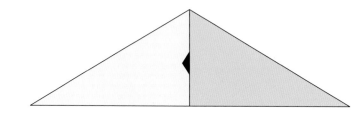

2. Repeat Step 1, using pairs of dark rectangles. Make 40 dark long half-triangles.

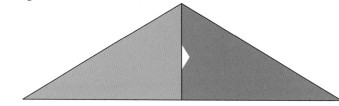

WORKING WITH BIAS

Long bias edges can cause the fabric to stretch too easily. Here are some tips that we have found to be helpful when working with bias edges.

- *Stabilize the fabric first before cutting the pieces. Use starch or starch alternatives (such as Magic Sizing or Mary Ellen's Best Press).*

- *Check that your sewing machine feeds the fabric through easily. If you find that the top layer of fabric is longer than the bottom after you've sewn a seam, or if the seam is significantly wavy, lessen the pressure on the presser foot.*

- *If the fabric does stretch, place the fabric on a surface it does not stick to and spritz it with water to let it draw back up to its original shape. Once the fabric is dry, press it flat and begin again.*

- *Marci's favorite tip: When pressing bias edges, have a piece of flannel on the ironing board to hold the bottom layer of fabric in place. This also helps keep fingers away from the iron.*

Piece the Quilt

1. Arrange the long half-triangles into a pleasing arrangement of values and colors. Sew the pieces into columns.

2. At the top of each column, unstitch the center seam of the top long half-triangle and sew the triangle half to the column's opposite end. Sew these columns together to make the finished quilt top.

3. Add the borders.

Finish the Quilt

Layer, quilt, and bind to complete your quilt. Here is one suggestion for quilting.

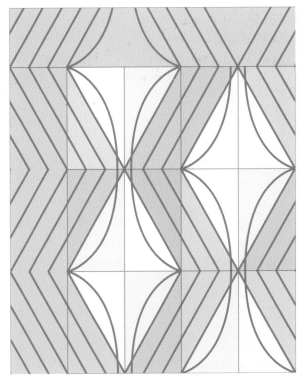

Quilting

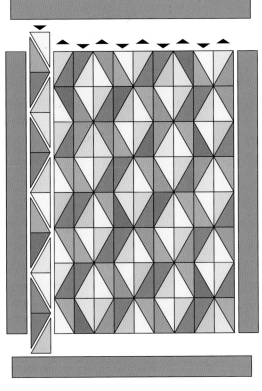

Piecing

TRIANGLES

These instructions use the Clearview Triangle or Clearview Super 60 ruler (see Tools, page 14). If you choose to work with patterns instead, see Patterns (page 124).

Cut Triangles

1. Cut a strip to the appropriate width for your project. (For this example we use a 3″ strip.) At the right end of the strip, place the ruler (or pattern) with a point up and any line aligned with the lower edge of the strip. Cut along the right edge of the ruler.

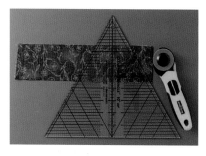

2. Turn the strip so that the angled end is to the left. With the ruler top-point-down and the left edge of the ruler at the left end of the strip, align the triangle size line (this is the same as the strip width, so 3″ here) along the top of the strip. Cut along the right side of the ruler.

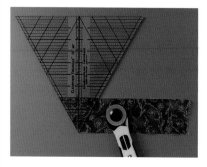

3. Rotate the ruler so that the top point is up and the triangle size line is now along the bottom of the strip. Cut. Repeat Steps 2 and 3 until you have the required number of triangles for your project.

4. To make sewing easier and faster at the machine, trim off the dog-ears at each corner before you remove the pieces from the mat (see Faster Alignment When Sewing, page 18). The triangles can be stacked when you trim the dog-ears.

Speed Piece Triangles

Whenever there is repetition in the design, you can speed piece the triangles.

1. Cut 2 strips to the appropriate width for your project. (Each project indicates the fabric combinations to sew.) With right sides together, sew these strips lengthwise down both sides. Cut triangles from this set of sewn strips (see Cut Triangles, at left).

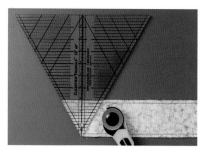

2. Pull the tips of the seamed triangles apart or trim the sewn tips using the Corner Cut 60 tool. It is not necessary to trim the other two corners. Press as indicated in the individual project.

Thousand Pyramids

Made by Annette Austin, machine quilted by Becky Marshall

Photo by Randy Pfizenmaier

▲ **Finished block:** 15" × 13"   ▲ **Finished quilt:** 60" × 78"

This pattern is created with dark and light triangles—and the different colors and prints cause larger pyramids to appear, too. This quilt certainly has the warm, traditional look that is so well loved. To simplify the piecing using Sara's process of piecing large triangle blocks, this pattern is one row shorter than the quilt shown.

YARDAGE

Light pyramid: ¼ yard of at least 14 fabrics **or** 16 fat quarters

Dark pyramid: ¼ yard of at least 14 fabrics **or** 16 fat quarters

Binding: ⅝ yard

Backing: 5 yards

Batting: 68″ × 86″

CUTTING

Light pyramid

* Cut a total of 28 strips 4″ × width of fabric. If using fat quarters, cut a total of 58 strips 4″ × 20″.

   Select 14 strips, one from each fabric. Square one end and cut 1 rectangle 4″ × 4½″ from each strip. Trim these 14 rectangles down to 2⅝″ × 4½″.

   Cut 7 rectangles into 14 left triangle halves, and cut the other 7 rectangles into 14 right triangle halves. (Refer to Cut Triangle Halves, page 23.) There will be 2 extra of each triangle for layout options.

* Cut the remaining strips into at least 372 triangles 4″ high. (Refer to Cut Triangles, page 32.)

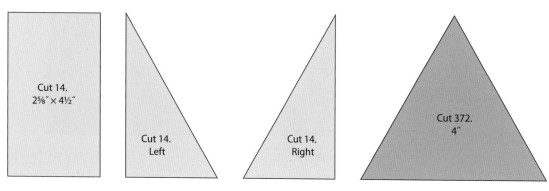

Cut 14.
2⅝″ × 4½″

Cut 14.
Left

Cut 14.
Right

Cut 372.
4″

Dark pyramid

- Cut a total of 28 strips 4″ × width of fabric. If using fat quarters, cut 58 strips 4″ × 20″.

  Select 14 strips, one from each fabric. Square one end and cut 1 rectangle 4″ × 4½″ from each strip. Trim these 14 rectangles down to 2⅝″ × 4½″.

  Cut 7 rectangles into 14 left triangle halves, and cut the other 7 rectangles into 14 right triangle halves. (Refer to Cut Triangle Halves, page 23.) There will be 2 extra of each triangle for layout options.

- Cut the remaining strips into at least 372 triangles 4″ high. (Refer to Cut Triangles, page 32.)

Binding

- Calculate the size needed for your style of binding (see Figure *Your* Binding Width, page 21). Cut 8 width-of-fabric strips in that size.

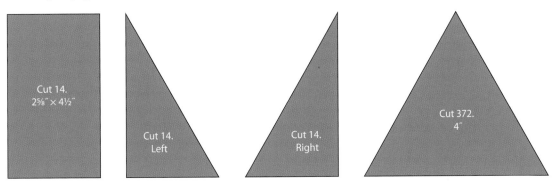

Cut 14.
2⅝″ × 4½″

Cut 14.
Left

Cut 14.
Right

Cut 372.
4″

CONSTRUCTION

Seam allowances are ¼″ unless otherwise noted.

Piece the Blocks

Follow the arrows for pressing direction.

Make the Dark Blocks (Dark Triangles Outside)

1. Arrange 10 dark and 6 light triangles to make 1 block.

2. Sew the triangles into rows. To reduce bulk at the seams, begin piecing each row at the arrow and press each seam in the direction of the arrow after each triangle is added. Sew the rows together and press the seams as shown.

3. Repeat Steps 1 and 2 to make a total of 24 dark blocks.

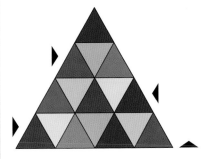

Make 24.

Make the Light Blocks (Light Triangles Outside)

1. Arrange 10 light and 6 dark triangles to make 1 block.

2. Sew the triangles into rows. To reduce bulk at the seams, begin piecing each row at the arrow and press each seam in the direction of the arrow after each triangle is added. Sew the rows together and press the seams as shown.

3. Repeat Steps 1 and 2 to make a total of 18 light blocks.

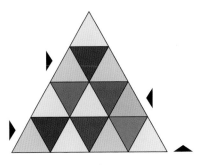

Make 18.

Make the Left Half-Blocks
(Left Edge of the Quilt)

1. Arrange the following pieces to make a left half-block: 4 light and 2 dark triangles, 2 light right triangle halves, and 2 dark left triangle halves.

2. Sew the triangles into rows. To reduce bulk at the seams, press the row after each triangle is added, pressing the seams in the direction of the arrows.

3. Sew the rows together and press the seams as shown.

4. Repeat Steps 1–3 to make a total of 6 left half-blocks.

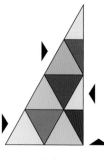

Make 6.

Make the Right Half-Blocks
(Right Edge of the Quilt)

1. Arrange the following pieces to make a right half-block: 4 light and 2 dark triangles, 2 light left triangle halves, and 2 dark right triangle halves.

2. Sew the triangles into rows. To reduce bulk at the seams, press the row after each triangle is added, pressing the seams in the direction of the arrows.

3. Sew the rows together and press the seams as shown.

4. Repeat Steps 1–3 to make a total of 6 right half-blocks.

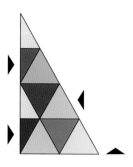

Make 6.

Piece the Quilt

1. Arrange the blocks and half-blocks to create a pleasing arrangement of values and colors. Be sure to put all the *dark blocks point up* and all the *light blocks point down*. That is what makes the design Thousand Pyramids.

2. Sew the blocks into rows. To reduce bulk at the seams, start at the end where the arrow is in the piecing diagram and press the seams in that direction after each block is added.

Piecing

Finish the Quilt

Layer, quilt, and bind to complete your quilt. Here is one suggestion for quilting that avoids the seam intersections.

Quilting

Thousand Pyramids Quick Quilt *by Sara Nephew, quilted by Judy Irish*

Large triangles of fabric make a quick, comfortable nap quilt. With a range of reds from light to dark, the grouped fabric placement brings interest to the design. This classic pattern is easy to make once you understand that the light triangles and dark triangles must point in opposite directions. Sewn using 10 light and 10 dark strips 6″ × width of fabric, 6″ triangle pairs, and speed-piecing techniques (see Speed Piece Triangles, page 32), this quilt made a fast and fun gift.

Rolling Ball

Made by Sara Nephew, quilted by Judy Irish

▲ **Finished block:** 9½″ × 8¼″   ▲ **Finished quilt:** 58¼″ × 63¾″

Sara chose a dramatic fabric that allowed her to cut stacked triangles to create hexagons. This technique is one of her favorites because the fabric does the work and provides serendipitous designs. So much fun!

To simplify the sewing process, Marci wrote the project instructions for a slightly larger quilt than Sara's original. The edges finish with full blocks. Keep this in mind when comparing the photo with the piecing diagram and your finished project.

YARDAGE

Medium to dark rolling balls: ¼ yard of 8 or more fabrics **or** 8 fat quarters (If a kaleidoscope look is desired, use 2 yards or 6 repeats of a high contrast large-scale print.)

Light background: ¼ yard of 11 or more fabrics **or** 11 fat quarters

Side accent/background: ⅜ yard

Border: ⅞ yard

Binding: ⅝ yard

Backing: 3¾ yards

Batting: 66″ × 72″

CUTTING

Medium to dark rolling balls

- *If using ¼ yards:* Cut a total of 15 strips 3½″ × width of fabric.

  From 5 full-width of fabric strips, cut a total of 90 triangles 3½″ high. (See Cut Triangles, page 32.) The remainder of the strips will be used in the next section.

- *If using fat quarters:* Cut 35 strips 3½″ × 20″.

  From 12 fat quarter strips, cut a total of 90 triangles 3½″ high. (See Cut Triangles, page 32.) The remainder of the strips will be used in the next section.

- *If using repeat fabric:* Stack the fabric according to the instructions in Stacked Repeats Resources (page 98).

  Depending on how the stacked fabric was cut, subcut 3 strips 3½″ × width of fabric or 6 strips 3½″ × 20″. Cut 45 stacks of triangles 3½″ high, with 6 triangles per stack.

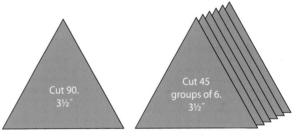

Light background

- Cut a total of 21 strips 3½″ × width of fabric. If using fat quarters, cut 46 strips 3½″ × 20″.

  From 11 width-of-fabric strips or 23 fat quarter strips, cut 182 triangles 3½″ high. The remainder of the strips will be used in the next section.

  If using repeat fabric, cut an additional 179 triangles 3½″ high.

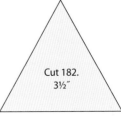

Cutting list continues…

Side accent/background

- Cut 1 strip 9½″ × width of fabric.

  Cut 7 rectangles 5½″ × 9½″. Subcut 6 left and 8 right triangle halves, following the directions in Cut Triangle Halves (page 23).

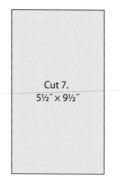

Cut 7.
5½″ × 9½″

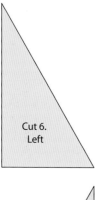

Cut 6.
Left

Cut 8.
Right

Border

- Cut 7 strips 3½″ × width of fabric.

Binding

- Calculate the size needed for your style of binding (see Figure *Your* Binding Width, page 21). Cut 7 width-of-fabric strips in that size.

CONSTRUCTION

Seam allowances are ¼″ unless otherwise noted.

Piece the Blocks

Follow the arrows for pressing direction.

Make the Triangle Pairs

Pair each light strip with a dark strip. Follow the directions in Speed Piece Triangles (page 32) to cut pairs of 3½″-high triangles. Make 179 pairs. Press half of the pairs toward the light side and half toward the dark.

If using repeat fabric, skip this step.

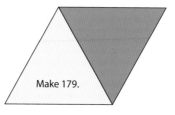

Make 179.

Make the Rolling Ball Units

1. Arrange 3 triangle pairs and 3 dark triangles to make 1 Triangle Block A. If using repeat fabric, make Block A with 1 stack of matching triangles and 3 light triangles. Sew the triangles together. Make a total of 10 blocks.

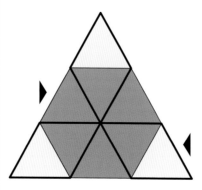

Block A: Make 10.

2. Arrange 2 triangle pairs, 1 dark triangle, and 4 light triangles to make 1 Triangle Block B. If using repeat fabric, make Block B with half of a stack of matching triangles and 6 light triangles. Save the other half of the stack for Block C. Sew the triangles together. Make a total of 31 blocks.

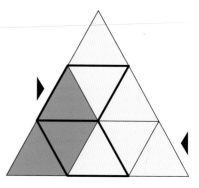

Block B: Make 31.

3. Use 3 triangle pairs, 1 dark triangle, and 2 light triangles to sew Triangle Block C. If using repeat fabric, make Block C from the other half of the stack from Block B (so a B and C will match) and 5 light triangles, noting that the single dark triangle is missing. Make a total of 29 blocks.

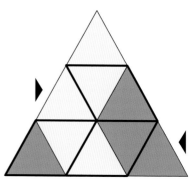

Block C: Make 29.

Piece the Quilt

1. Arrange Triangle Blocks A, B, and C to determine the best placement. If using stacked repeats, this arrangement includes placing the remaining triangle stacks. Once you are pleased with your placement, sew the single triangles onto the C blocks.

2. Sew the triangle blocks into rows. As you sew, pinch wherever four seams come together, peek at their alignment, and pin all along the two rows. (For more details, see Tip: Pin the Points, page 58.) Sew the rows together to complete the quilt top. Press the long seams in one direction.

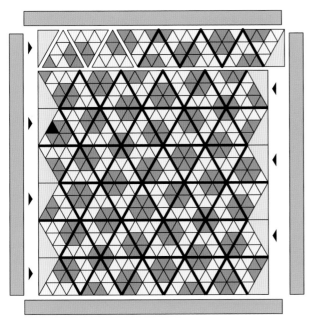

Piecing

3. Add the borders.

Finish the Quilt

Layer, quilt, and bind to complete your quilt. For stacked repeats, add individual quilting designs at the center of each rolling ball. Here is one suggestion for quilting that avoids the seam intersections.

Quilting

Meteorite

Made by Sara Nephew, quilted by Judy Irish

▲ **Finished quilt:** 53″ × 68½″

These balls look like they are floating in space—hence the name Meteorite. *Use a dark, strong-colored fabric for the balls and light-colored prints for the background to achieve this floating effect. Choose fabrics that are pleasing to you. In this quilt Sara used both regular quilting-weight fabric and scraps of decorator fabric to obtain a variety of textures and patterns.*

YARDAGE

Medium to dark meteorites: ¼ yard of 13–15 fabrics **or** 10 or 11 fat quarters

Light background: ¼ yard of 17–19 fabrics **or** 13 or 14 fat quarters

Border: 1⅛ yards

Binding: ⅝ yard

Backing: 3½ yards

Batting: 61″ × 76″

CUTTING

Medium to dark meteorites

- If using ¼ yards, cut a total of 13 strips 4½″ × width of fabric. If using fat quarters, cut 30 strips 4½″ × 20″.

  Select 4 strips to use for filling in edges at top and bottom. Cut 2 triangles 4½″ high from each of these 4 strips.

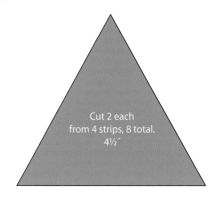

Cut 2 each
from 4 strips, 8 total.
4½″

Light background

- If using ¼ yards, cut a total of 17 strips 4½″ × width of fabric. If using fat quarters, cut 36 strips 4½″ × 20″.

  Select 8 strips to use for filling in edges at top and bottom. Cut 2 triangles 4½″ high from each of these 8 strips.

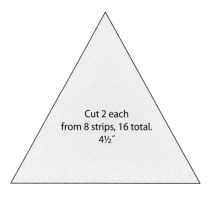

Cut 2 each
from 8 strips, 16 total.
4½″

Border

- Cut 7 strips 4½″ × width of fabric.

Binding

- Calculate the size needed for your style of binding (see Figure *Your* Binding Width, page 21). Cut 7 width-of-fabric strips in that size.

CONSTRUCTION

Seam allowances are ¼″ unless otherwise noted.

Piece the Blocks

Press toward the darker fabric.

Make the Triangle Pair Units

With the remaining strips, sew and cut triangle pairs following the directions in Speed Piece Triangles (page 32). Make 72 light/light pairs, 48 light/dark pairs, and 48 dark/dark pairs.

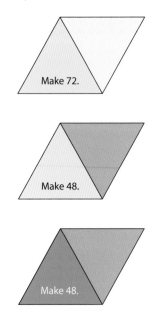

Piece the Quilt

There are many ways to sew this quilt together. Two such methods are presented here.

Method One

This method gives the most flexibility for fabric placement.

1. Arrange all triangle pairs and single triangles in a pleasing design.

2. Continue with the steps listed under For Both Methods (next page).

Method Two

Work with long units, repeating and shifting the pattern throughout the design as you would for a Bargello quilt. This is achieved by sewing multiples of the long unit and then splitting some of the units at the specified seam needed for the design.

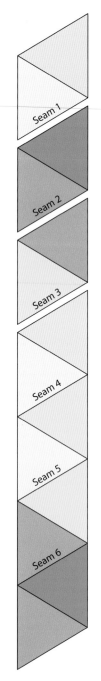

Make 24 long units for quick piecing.

1. Arrange 3 light/light pairs, 2 light/dark pairs, and 2 dark/dark pairs. Sew one long unit. Make a total of 24 units.

2. Set aside 14 complete units. Unstitch the remaining units at the indicated seam. Position the partial units as shown in the piecing diagram (below) so that the unstitched seam is at the top or bottom of the quilt.

3. Add in light (L) and dark (D) single triangles at the top and bottom as shown.

4. Continue with the steps listed under For Both Methods.

For Both Methods

1. Sew triangle pairs or units into columns. As you sew, pinch wherever four seams come together, peek at their alignment, and pin all along the two rows. (For more details, see Tip: Pin the Points, page 58.)

2. Sew the columns together to complete the quilt top. Press the long seams in one direction. Trim where the triangles extend at the top and bottom, leaving ¼" seam allowance.

Piecing

3. Add the borders.

Finish the Quilt

Layer, quilt, and bind to complete your quilt. Here are two suggestions for quilting that avoid the seam intersections.

Quilting

Fantasy

Made by Kathy Syring, quilted by Judy Irish

Photo by Randy Pfizenmaier

▲ **Finished block:** 15¾" × 13½"   ▲ **Finished quilt:** 71" × 89"

Thoughtful placement of soft color combinations and strong contrasting colors create a quilt that simultaneously draws and rests the eye. It is not just geometry!

YARDAGE

Light (peach): 1¼ yards

Light medium (pale green): ⅝ yard

Medium 1 (multicolor): 2 yards

Medium 2 (turquoise): ¾ yard

Medium 3 (brown): ⅞ yard

Medium dark (fuchsia): 1⅛ yards

Dark (navy): 2¼ yards

Border (navy): 1¼ yards

Binding: ¾ yard

Backing: 5½ yards

Batting: 79″ × 97″

CUTTING

Triangle fabrics

- Cut the following 3″ × width of fabric strips from the designated fabrics:

	Light (L)	Medium light (ML)	Medium 1 (M1)	Medium 2 (M2)	Medium 3 (M3)	Medium dark (MD)	Dark (D)
Cut 3″ strips.	13	6	22	7	8	11	15

From these strips, cut the following number of 3″-high triangles only from the designated fabrics:

	Light (L)	Medium 3 (M3)	Medium dark (MD)	Dark (D)
Cut 3″ triangles.	48	24	48	24

- Cut the rest of the triangles, following the instructions in Speed Piece Triangles (page 32). The number of strip pairs for each pair of fabrics, the number of 3″ triangle pairs to cut from the strips, and the direction in which the seam should be pressed are shown in the table below.

	Light (L) medium 1 (ML1)	Light (L) and medium dark (MD)	Medium 1 (M1) and dark (D)	Medium 1 (M1) and medium 2 (M2)	Medium light (ML) and medium 3 (M3)
Sew strip pairs.	2	8	13	7	6
Cut 3″ triangle pairs.	24	168	264	144	120
Fabric to press toward	Light	Half toward medium dark and half toward light	Medium 1	Medium 1	Medium light

Edge pieces

- Cut 8 strips 3½″ × width of fabric from the dark fabric.

  From these strips, cut 144 rectangles 2″ × 3½″. (Refer to Cut Triangle Halves, page 23.) Subcut these into 144 left and 144 right triangle halves.

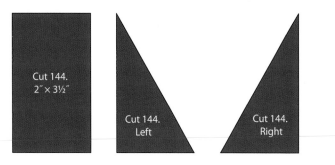

Cut 144.
2″ × 3½″

Cut 144.
Left

Cut 144.
Right

Border

- Cut 8 strips 4½″ × width of fabric.

Binding

- Calculate the size needed for your style of binding (see Figure *Your* Binding Width, page 21). Cut 9 width-of-fabric strips in that size.

CONSTRUCTION

Seam allowances are ¼″ unless otherwise noted.

Piece the Blocks

Follow the arrows for pressing direction.

Make the Fantasy Blocks

1. Arrange the Fantasy blocks, following the diagram. Note how the single triangles fit into the design by alternating them at the end of the row.

2. Sew the triangle pairs, single triangles, and triangle halves into horizontal rows. To reduce bulk at the seams, begin piecing each row at the arrow and press each seam in the direction of the arrow after each triangle is added. Then sew these together to make the block. Make 12 Fantasy blocks.

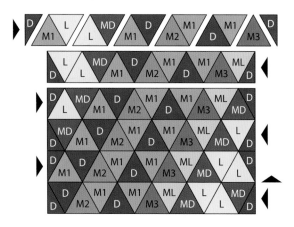

Make the Reverse Fantasy Blocks

1. Arrange the Reverse Fantasy block, following the diagram.

2. Sew and press in the same manner as the Fantasy block. Make 12 Reverse Fantasy blocks.

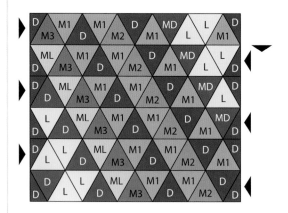

Piece the Quilt

1. Arrange the blocks and reverse blocks, alternating them in one row and rotating them in the next row.

2. Sew the blocks into rows, and then sew the rows together to complete the top.

3. Add the borders.

Piecing

Finish the Quilt

Layer, quilt, and bind to complete your quilt. Here are several suggestions for quilting that avoid the seam intersections and highlight the radiating design.

Quilting

VARIATIONS

Fantasy Variation *by Deborah Haynes*
Photo by Randy Pfizenmaier

Deb selected a bright and cheerful mix of colors to bring out this strong design. The light-blue inner border and the additional dark borders keep all the action contained. With 4″ cut triangles and only 12 blocks, her finished quilt was 68″ × 78½″, similar in size to the original.

Diamond in the Rough *by Marci Baker*

Marci wanted to try out some color ideas in this truncated version of the *Fantasy* pattern. These radiant colors would look beautiful in a full-sized quilt. Marci used 5¾″-high triangles and 3⅝″ × 6¼″ rectangles for triangle halves in order to make this fast and fun quilt that is 52″ × 60″.

DIAMONDS AND LONG DIAMONDS

Cut Diamonds

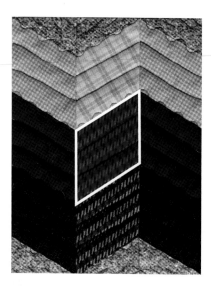

1. Cut a strip the appropriate width for your project. (For this example we use a 3″ strip.) At the right end of the strip, place the ruler with one side or line aligned with the lower edge of the strip. Cut along the right edge of the ruler to get a 60° angle.

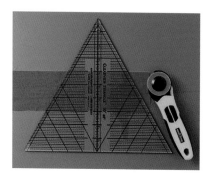 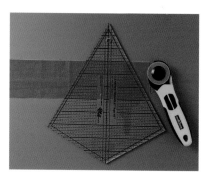

These instructions use the Clearview Triangle or Clearview Super 60 ruler (see Tools, page 14). If you choose to work with patterns instead, see Patterns (page 124).

2. Turn the strip with the angled end to the left.

If using the Clearview Triangle ruler: Place the ruler at the left end of the strip so that the top point is at the lower left and the ¼″ line is along the bottom of the strip. Align the appropriate ruler line, as measured from the bottom of the ruler with the cut end of the strip, to cut the diamond the same width as the strip. (The example shown is a 3″ diamond.) Cut along the right side of the ruler.

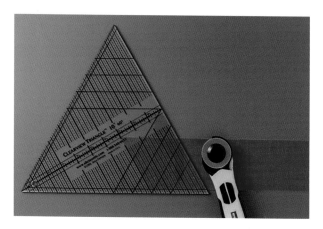

If using the Clearview Super 60 ruler: Place the ruler top-point-up so that the edge of the ruler is at the lower left corner and the ruler line for your chosen diamond size is at the bottom edge of the strip. (The example shown is a 3″ diamond.) Cut *only* on the right side of the ruler.

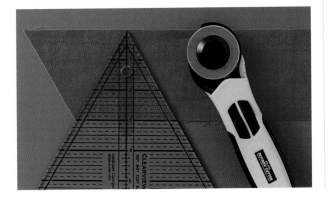

3. Continue cutting until you have the required number of diamonds.

4. *Optional:* Trim dog-ears off at both ends to make the sewing easier and faster.

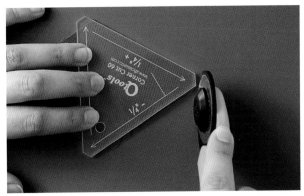

Cut Long Diamonds

LEFT

1. Cut a strip to the appropriate width for your project. Place the ruler with a point facing up and a line aligned with the lower edge of the strip. Cut along the right edge of the ruler.

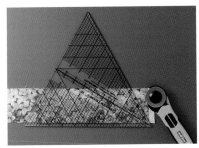
Using Clearview Triangle ruler

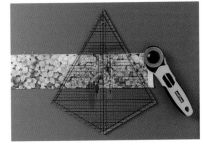
Using Clearview Super 60 ruler

2. Turn the strip with the angled end to the left. Note how this cut end leans to the left.

If using the Clearview Triangle ruler: Place the ruler at the left end of the strip so that the top point is at the lower left and the ¼″ line is along the bottom of the strip. Align the appropriate ruler line, as measured from the bottom of the ruler (6″ is shown here), with the cut end of the strip. Cut the long diamond.

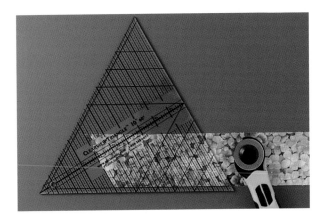

If using the Clearview Super 60 ruler: Place the ruler at the left end with the top point up. Align the appropriate ruler line (measured from the top of the ruler) with the bottom edge of the strip. Also align the left edge of the ruler to match the lower left corner of the strip. Make the cut only on the right side of the ruler.

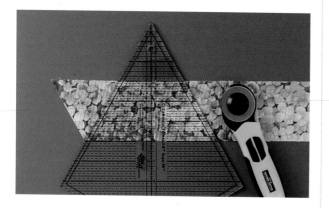

3. Repeat this process to cut the necessary number of left long diamonds.

4. *Optional:* Trim dog-ears off both ends to make the sewing easier and faster.

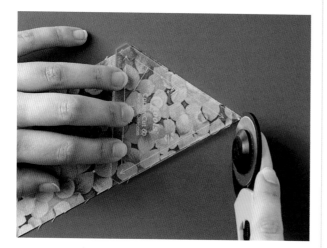

RIGHT

1. Cut a strip to the appropriate width for your project. At the right end of the strip, place the ruler with a point facing down and a line aligned with the upper edge of the strip. Cut along the right edge of the ruler.

Using Clearview Triangle ruler

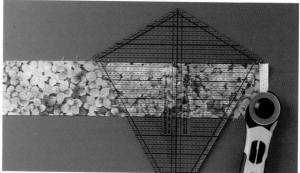

Using Clearview Super 60 ruler

2. Turn the strip with the angled end to the left. Note how this cut end leans to the right.

If using the Clearview Triangle ruler: Place the ruler at the left end of the strip so that the top point is at the upper left and the ¼" line is along the top of the strip. Align the appropriate ruler line, as measured from the bottom of the ruler (6" is shown here), with the cut end of the strip. Cut the long diamond.

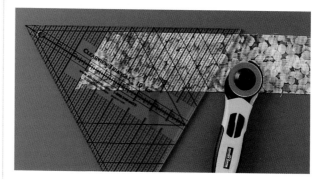

If using the Clearview Super 60 ruler: Place the ruler at the left end with the top point down. Align the appropriate ruler line (measured from the top of the ruler) with the top edge of the strip. Also align the left edge of the ruler to match the upper left corner of the strip. Make the cut only on the right side of the ruler.

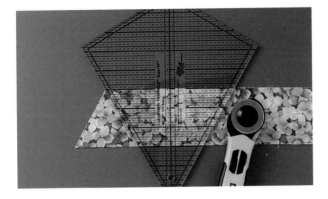

3. Repeat this process to cut the necessary number of right long diamonds.

4. *Optional:* Trim dog-ears off both ends to make the sewing easier and faster.

tip

STACKING LEFT AND RIGHT DIAMONDS

Cut both left and right long diamonds at the same time by stacking the strips. Place the right fabric wrong side up and then stack the left fabric on top, right side up. After arranging the stack, follow the instructions for cutting left long diamonds (page 51).

Cut Diamond Halves

WITH THE CLEARVIEW SUPER 60 RULER

1. With the strip in a vertical position, align the width-of-strip ruler line along the left edge of the fabric and the bottom point of the Clearview Super 60 ruler on the right edge of the fabric. Cut along both edges of the Clearview Super 60 ruler. This will trim the end and make a diamond half.

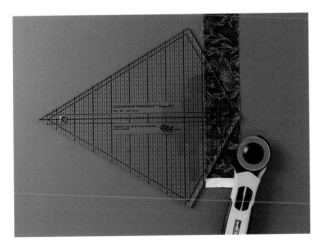

2. Position the ruler again on the left side, aligning the lower edge with the lower left point of the strip. Cut along both edges of the Clearview Super 60 ruler, resulting in two additional diamond halves. Repeat this process to cut the necessary number of diamond halves.

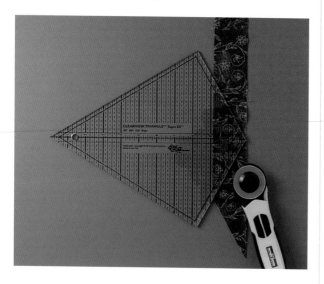

WITH THE CLEARVIEW TRIANGLE RULER

1. With the strip in a vertical position, align the ruler so that the point is down, toward you, and the center line is along the left edge of the strip. Cut along the right edge of the ruler.

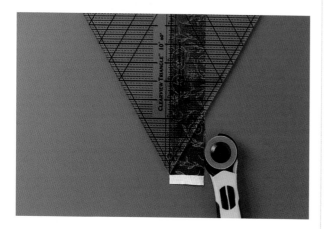

2. Rotate the ruler so the point is up, away from you; the center line is along the left edge of the strip; and the right edge of the ruler is at the lower right corner of the strip (as determined from the previous cut). Cut along the right edge of the ruler. The size of your strip determines the size of the diamond half.

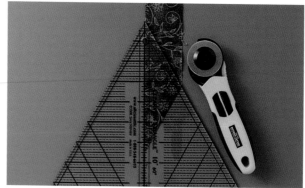

3. Repeat Steps 1 and 2 to cut the necessary number of diamond halves.

Cut Strata of Diamonds/ Long Diamonds

LEFT

1. Use the sewn left strip set given in any project that has the top strip shifted to the left of any lower strips. At the right end of the strip, place the ruler so that the point is up and the ¼" line is aligned with the lower edge of the strip. Cut along the right edge of the ruler.

2. Turn the strip around. Place the ruler at the left end, with the top point to the lower left and the ¼" line along the bottom of the strip. Align the appropriate ruler line, measured from the bottom of the ruler, with the cut end of the strip. (In the example shown, the measurement is 3".) Cut the left strata.

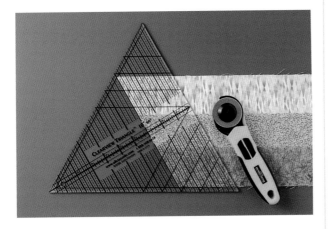

If you are using the Clearview Super 60 ruler, use a regular ruler to measure and cut the widths in this step. Check the 60° angle often, using the Clearview Super 60 ruler. If it does not align, repeat Step 1 to reestablish the 60° angle.

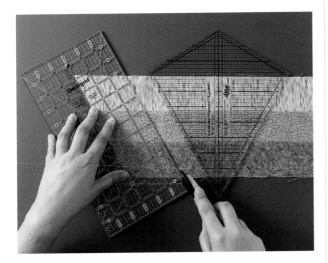

RIGHT

1. Use the sewn right strip set given in any project that has the top strip shifted to the right of any lower strips. At the right end of the strip, place the ruler so that the point is down and the ¼" line is aligned with the upper edge of the strip. Cut along the right edge of the ruler.

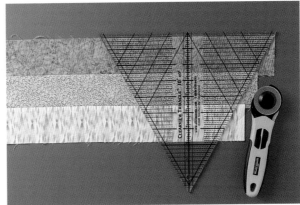

2. Turn the strip around. Place the ruler at the left end, with the top point to the upper left and the ¼" line along the top of the strip. Align the appropriate ruler line measured from the bottom of the ruler with the cut end of the strip. (In the example, 3" is shown.) Cut the right strata.

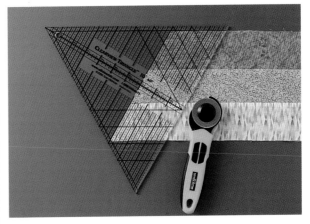

If using the Clearview Super 60 ruler, use a regular ruler to measure and cut the widths in this step in the same manner as the left strata. Check the 60° angle often, using the Clearview Super 60 ruler. If it does not align, repeat Step 1 to reestablish the 60° angle.

Casino

Made by Sarah Ann Newman

Photo by Randy Pfizenmaier

◢ **Finished block:** 11¾" × 13½"   ◢ **Finished quilt:** 30½" × 34"

The shapes in this design can be rearranged and reformed to suit the will of the quilter. Put the diamonds on a design wall and move them into a different pattern. This makes for endless possibilities, and it is easy to find winning combinations. Sew together four of the same panel to create a great wallhanging that is uniquely yours!

YARDAGE

Diamonds: ¼ yard each of the following:

  3 light fabrics A, B, and C (peach, yellow, and green)

  1 medium fabric D (pink)

  3 dark fabrics E, F, and G (red, green, and multicolor)

Border 1 (black): ¼ yard

Border 2 (multicolor batik): ½ yard

Binding: ⅜ yard

Backing: 1¼ yards

Batting: 38″ × 42″

CUTTING

Diamonds and Triangles

In keeping with the creative spirit of this design, the instructions call for a generous amount of cut pieces. Place, rearrange, and move these pieces around on a design wall until your desired effect is achieved. If needed, more pieces can be cut.

- Cut 2 strips 2¾″ × width of fabric from each of the 7 fabrics.

  From each pair of fabric strips, subcut the following: 15 diamonds 2¾″, according to the instructions in Cut Diamonds (page 50) and 5 triangles 3″ high, according to the instructions in Cut Triangles (page 32). (*Note: These triangles will have their top tip missing because the strip is ¼″ narrower than usual. This is fine because the difference is hidden in the seam allowance.*)

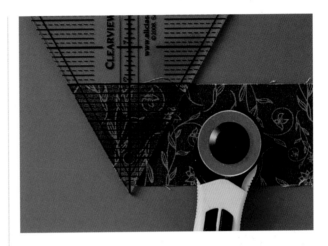

From the center diamond fabrics, select 2 different fabric strips. Cut 2 rectangles 2″ × 3½″ for the triangle halves. Set the rectangles aside.

- Cut down the remaining strips to 1⅞″ strips. Cut 4 diamond halves 1⅞″ from each fabric, according to the instructions in Cut Diamond Halves (page 53).

Borders

- *Border 1:* Cut 4 strips 1″ × width of fabric.

- *Border 2:* Cut 4 strips 3½″ × width of fabric.

Binding

- Calculate the size needed for your style of binding (see Figure *Your* Binding Width, page 21). Cut 4 width-of-fabric strips in that size.

CONSTRUCTION

Press all seams in each strip in one direction.

Piece the Blocks

Make the Casino Block

1. Arrange the pieces in the values shown, using light fabrics for A, B, and C; medium fabric for D; and dark fabrics for E, F, and G; *or alter the arrangement as desired.* Use cut diamonds and triangles to fill in at the edges and center.

2. Once satisfied with the design placement, cut left and right triangle halves from the reserved 2″ × 3½″ rectangles for the corners, following the instructions in Cut Triangle Halves (page 23).

3. Sew the pieces into diagonal rows, following the piecing diagram (below left). (To sew the diagonal rows successfully, pin the points so they match exactly before sewing the rows together. See Tip: Pin the Points, below.)

4. Repeat Steps 1 and 3 to create a second Casino block.

···· *tip* ····

PIN THE POINTS ⟋ by Marci

To match points precisely, here is a pinning method I learned early on in my quilting career. Place the fabric pieces right sides together and put a pin through both at the points that are to match. Make sure the pin is perpendicular to the pieces of fabric.

Pin on both sides, without twisting the fabric. The first pin should still be perpendicular, showing that the two points are still aligned.

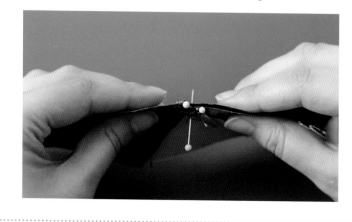

Make the Reverse Casino Blocks

Using a Casino block as a reference, create 2 Reverse Casino blocks. (An easy way to do this is to check the reversed blocks from left to right while reading the Casino block from right to left.) Sew the Reverse Casino block pieces together in diagonal rows, following the instructions in Make the Casino Block (page 58). Sew the rows together to complete each block.

Piece the Quilt

Note: The design comprises 2 Casino blocks and 2 Reverse Casino blocks.

Piecing

1. Arrange the 4 blocks to make the final quilt. Note that the bottom half is the same as the top half, just rotated 180°. Sew the sections together to see the final design. Twist the seams if needed to reduce bulk.

2. Add the borders.

3. Repeat Step 2 with the 3½″ strips for Border 2.

Finish the Quilt

Layer, quilt, and bind to complete your quilt. Here is one suggestion for quilting that avoids the seam intersections.

Quilting

These blocks can produce even more patterns and designs by repeating them to make a larger quilt. Here is a preview of what this block could look like as a throw-size quilt.

The blocks are 11¾" × 13½" finished. This variation features four times as many blocks as the original pattern; with 8 Casino blocks and 8 Reverse Casino blocks, the finished quilt measures 47" × 54" before borders. The yardage for this larger project is ¾ yard each of 7 different fabrics. Add extra fabric if your design emphasizes one fabric more than the others. For a 6" border (cut at 6½"), the project needs 1⅜ yards.

Sara made this dramatic wallhanging using a variety of fabrics that shimmer across the surface. This variation adds triangles with the diamonds. To replicate the look, just cut a lot of diamonds from interesting fabrics and place them into vertical rows. Occasionally, a triangle is inserted to change the direction of the row. (You could sew a diamond in sideways and trim it even with the edge of the row, if you prefer.) Interesting patterns and colors—maybe even a little metallic flash in the fabric—make an artistic composition.

Glitter Leaves by Sara Nephew, quilted by Judy Irish

Don't Tread on Me

Made by Marci Baker

 Finished block: 12" × 12"   Finished quilt: 48" × 60"

This is a great framed piece for someone's office because of the strong graphic design. The construction is simple and there is plenty of color, value, and texture to catch the eye.

YARDAGE

Medium and dark of 3 colorways (gray, red, and white): ⅜ yard each of 6 fabrics (2 of each colorway)

Edges (medium gray): ⅜ yard

Border (medium gray): 1⅜ yards

Binding: ½ yard

Backing: 3¼ yards

Batting: 56″ × 68″

CUTTING

Gradations

- Cut 3 strips 3½″ × width of fabric from each of the 6 fabrics.

Edge fabric

- Cut 5 strips 2¼″ × width of fabric

  Subcut into 48 rectangles 2¼″ × 4″. Cut 48 left and 48 right triangle halves, following the instructions in Cut Triangle Halves (page 23).

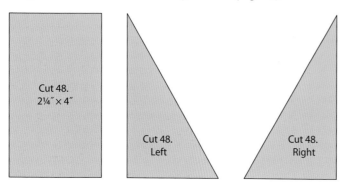

Cut 48.
2¼″ × 4″

Cut 48.
Left

Cut 48.
Right

Border

- Cut 6 strips 6½″ × width of fabric.

Binding

- Calculate the size needed for your style of binding (see Figure *Your* Binding Width, page 21). Cut 6 width-of-fabric strips in that size.

CONSTRUCTION

Seam allowances are ¼" unless otherwise noted.

Piece the Blocks

Follow the arrows for pressing direction.

Piece the Strip Sets

Determine the order of the 2 sets (medium and dark) of 3 fabrics. Make a swatch card, if needed, to keep track of the order.

LEFT STRIP SET

Using a dark strip of each of the 3 colorways, sew a left strip set, staggering the strips so that the end of the bottom strip is slightly less than 2" below the end of the top strip. Pin the strips in place, because the bottom strip may slip. Sew a total of 3 left strip sets.

RIGHT STRIP SET

Using a medium strip of each of the 3 colorways, sew a right strip set, staggering the strips so that the top strip is slightly less than 2" below the edge of the bottom strip. Sew a total of 3 right strip sets.

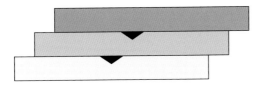

Cut and Piece Strata Together into a Block

1. Cut 3½" strata of diamonds, following the instructions in Cut Strata of Diamonds / Long Diamonds (page 54). Cut 24 left and 24 right strata of diamonds.

2. Using 2 left and 2 right strata of diamonds and 4 left and 4 right triangle halves of edge fabric, piece the block together. The seams should lock in place, making the points come together easily. Make 12 blocks.

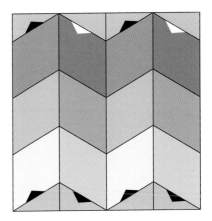

Piece the Quilt

1. Arrange the blocks as shown, or play with them to make your own variation. Sew the blocks into rows, and then sew the rows together to complete the quilt top.

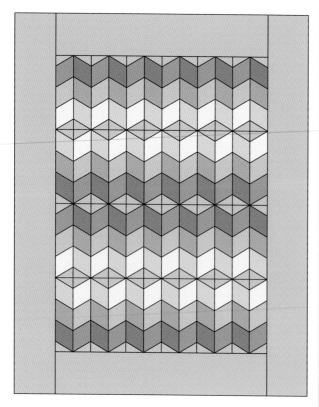

Piecing

2. Add the borders.

Finish the Quilt

Layer, quilt, and bind to complete your quilt. Here is one suggestion for quilting that avoids the seam intersections.

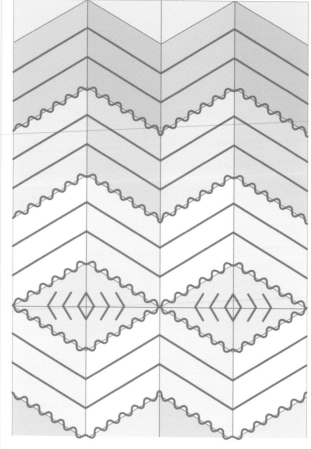

Quilting

Country Road

Made by Susan Porretta Weigner

Photo by Randy Pfizenmaier

✒ **Finished block:** 12″ × 12″   ✒ **Finished quilt:** 76″ × 88″

It's a lucky person who gets this quilt. Rich colors and careful planning bring out the pattern's movement and give it the feel of a folk art masterpiece. This is a road to travel on!

YARDAGE

Light to dark gradations (green, red to gold, and brown): 1 yard each of 9 fabrics (3 of each color)

Edges (dark brown): 1¼ yards

Border: ¾ yard

Binding: ¾ yard

Backing: 7 yards

Batting: 84" × 96"

CUTTING

Gradations

- From each of the 9 fabrics, cut 20 strips 1½" × width of fabric.

Edges

- Cut 17 strips 2¼" × width of fabric.

  Subcut 168 rectangles 2¼" × 4". Cut into 168 left and 168 right triangle halves, following the instructions in Cut Triangle Halves (page 23).

Cut 168. 2¼" × 4"

Cut 168. Left

Cut 168. Right

Border

- Cut 9 strips 2½" × width of fabric.

Binding

- Calculate the size needed for your style of binding (see Figure *Your* Binding Width, page 21). Cut 9 width-of-fabric strips in that size.

CONSTRUCTION

Seam allowances are ¼" unless otherwise noted.

Piece the Blocks

Follow the arrows for pressing direction.

Piece the Strip Sets

Determine the order (light to dark) of the 9 fabrics in the blocks. Make a swatch card, if needed, to keep track of the order. Refer to Straighter Seams, Less Ripping, Better Points— One Solution! (page 67) for tips on how to easily and consistently sew straight seams.

Straighter Seams, Less Ripping, Better Points— One Solution! ○— *by Marci*

Early in my sewing and quilting life, I struggled to sew straight strips. I had tried attaching moleskin fabric to the bed of my sewing machine to use as a guide, but the foam wore out, and the adhesive left a sticky mess. Now I use Sewing Edge—Reusable Vinyl Stops for Your Machine (available from C&T Publishing), which is a vinyl strip with repositionable adhesive. The more I have used this tool, the more I've realized how much I benefit from it.

* Sewing Edge is as thick as three layers of fabric, so as I sew I can feel that the fabric is aligned and not over the edge. It is a physical stop rather than a visual one, so I can guide the fabric by feel while letting the machine and Sewing Edge do the work.

* Because I watch my fabric well in front of the foot, if the strips are not lined up, I can fix them and keep sewing.

* When joining piecework to get a great point on the front, I sometimes need to take more than the normal seam allowance. For "perfect" points on the front, I hide things on the back. Unlike the quarter-inch sewing machine foot with an attached edge or the thicker stops offered for sewing machines, the Sewing Edge allows this extra bit of fabric to flow over the edge while still providing the $1/4$" seam allowance guide.

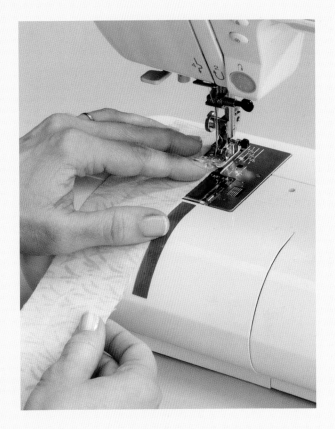

LEFT STRIP SET

1. Using a strip of each fabric, sew a left strip set, staggering the strips so that the end of the bottom strip is slightly less than 1″ below the end of the top strip. Pin this strip in place, because the bottom strip may slip.

2. To avoid a curved strip set, sew the strips in pairs first. Press all seams down.

3. Sew the pairs together; then sew the successive groups and last strip together, pressing the seams down.

4. Repeat Steps 1–3 to make a total of 10 left strip sets.

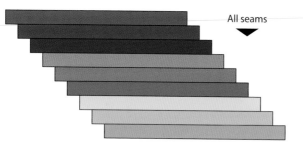

All seams

RIGHT STRIP SET

1. Using a strip of each fabric, sew a right strip set, staggering the strips so that the end of the top strip is slightly less than 1″ below the end of the bottom strip.

2. Sew the strips in pairs first. Press all seams up.

3. Sew the pairs together and the successive groups and last strip together, pressing the seams toward fabric 1.

4. Repeat Steps 1–3 to make a total of 10 right strip sets.

All seams

Cut and Piece Strata from Strip Sets

1. Cut 3½″ strata of long diamonds, following the instructions in Cut Strata of Diamonds / Long Diamonds (page 54). Cut 84 left and 84 right strata units.

2. Using 2 left and 2 right strata of long diamonds and 4 left and 4 right triangle halves of edge fabric, piece the block together. The seams should lock in place, making the points come together easily. Make a total of 42 blocks.

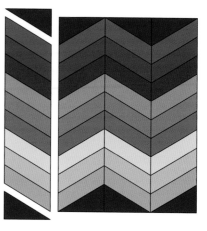

Piece the Quilt

1. Arrange the blocks as desired. Follow the piecing diagram, try a symmetrical design, or even place blocks randomly. Once your pattern is decided, sew the blocks into rows.

2. Sew rows together to complete the quilt top.

3. Add the borders.

Finish the Quilt

Layer, quilt, and bind to complete your quilt. Here is one suggestion for quilting that avoids the seam intersections.

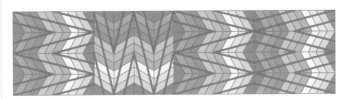

Quilting

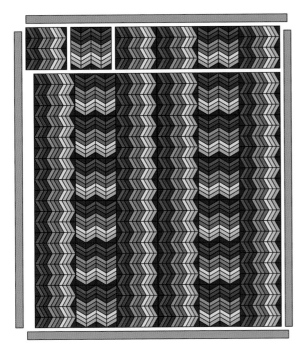

Piecing

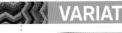 **VARIATIONS**

Country Road Baby Quilt Variation *by Sara Nephew*

Two layers of rich flannel make this a wondrously soft baby quilt. Sara played with sewn sets of strips and made the roads travel in different directions. It is a strong design with interesting details. This quilt uses the same-size strips as the main pattern, but it needs only 2 left and 2 right strip sets. Sara had an easy time getting this project made quickly for the baby to enjoy.

HALF-HEXAGONS

These instructions use the Clearview Triangle or Clearview Super 60 ruler (see Tools, page 14). If you choose to work with patterns instead, see Patterns (page 124).

Cut Half-Hexagons (a.k.a. Trapezoids)

1. Cut a strip to the appropriate width for your project. (For this example we use a 3″ strip.) At the right end of the strip, place the ruler so that a point is up and the lower ¼″ line is aligned with the lower edge of the strip. Cut along right edge of the ruler.

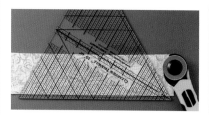

2. Turn the strip with the angled end to the left. With the point of the ruler facing down, align the half-hexagon size line along the top edge of the strip and left edge of the ruler along the left edge of the strip. (The example shows 5″ trapezoid cut from a 3″ strip.) Cut along the edge of the ruler.

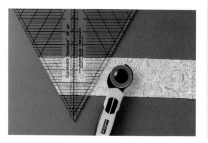

3. Rotate the ruler, align the size line along the bottom edge, and cut along the edge of the ruler. Continue cutting trapezoids until you have the number needed for your project.

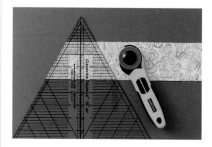

4. *Optional:* Trim the dog-ears off both ends to make the sewing easier and faster.

Fast Cut Half-Hexagons

1. Cut a strip to the appropriate width for your project. (For this example we use a 7″ strip.) At the right end of the strip, place the ruler so that the point is facing up and the ruler line is aligned with the lower edge of the strip. (To get the most out of the strip, slide the ruler sideways until the right edge is just above the center point of the end of the strip. This is approximate.) Cut along the right edge of the ruler.

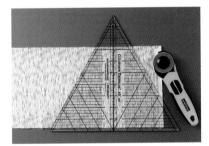

2. Turn the strip with angled end to the left. Cut slices the width of your desired half-hexagon, aligning the appropriate rule line along the angled end and keeping the ¼″ line along the bottom edge of the strip. The example shows 2½″ slices.

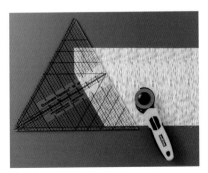

3. With the slice positioned horizontally, align the rule line for your given project along the bottom edge of the fabric, with the left edge of the ruler along the left edge of the slice. Before cutting, check that the shape under the ruler and the shape not under the ruler are equal to each other. Cut along the right side of the ruler. The first partial slice will only yield 1 half-hexagon.

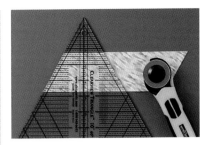

4. *Optional:* Trim the dog-ears off both ends to sew easier and faster.

Speed Piece Half-Hexagons

note

I use the term "hexalongs" for my speed-pieced half-hexagons. **by Marci**

1. Pair strips together as directed by the project instructions. Most often, half the pairs are shifted left and half are shifted right. Sew together along a long edge and press as noted in the project.

2. At the right end of the strip, align the ruler so that the point is up (for left-shifted strips) or down (for right-shifted strips). Align any rule line with the center seam (the longer the line, the better). Trim off the least amount of fabric you can to establish the 60° angle. The example shows 2 strips 3″ wide sewn together.

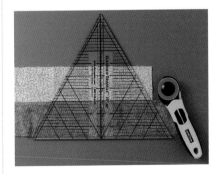

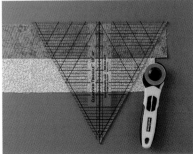

3. Turn the strip with the angled end to the left. Align the triangle ruler so that the slice width (which here is 1¾″) is measured along the cut edge to the left. If using the Clearview Super 60 ruler, use a regular 6″ × 12″ ruler to measure the slice width and the Clearview Super 60 ruler to verify that the angle is staying true. Cut the slice along the edge of the ruler.

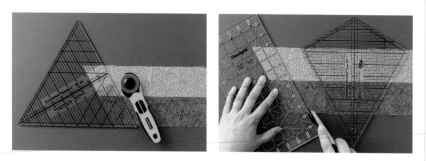

4. With the slice positioned horizontally, align the rule line for your project (3¼″ is shown) along the bottom of the fabric (for left-shifted; the point of the ruler is up) or along the top (for right-shifted; the point of the ruler is down). Also, have the ¼″ line aligned with the seam. *Note: There is a ¼″ triangle missing in the outer corner under the ruler.* Cut the triangle off at the right side, rotate the slice, and position the ruler the same way as before to cut off the triangle. Verify that the shape is cut correctly using the actual-size speed-pieced half-hexagon drawing.

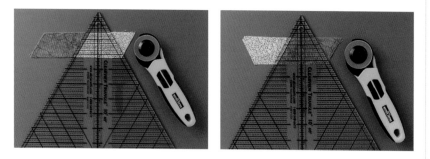

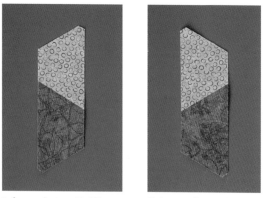

Left speed-pieced half-hexagon   Right speed-pieced half-hexagon

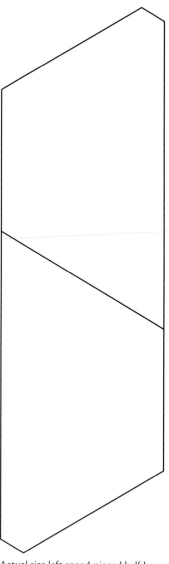

Actual size left speed-pieced half-hexagon drawing. Place wrong side up for right.

Gumball

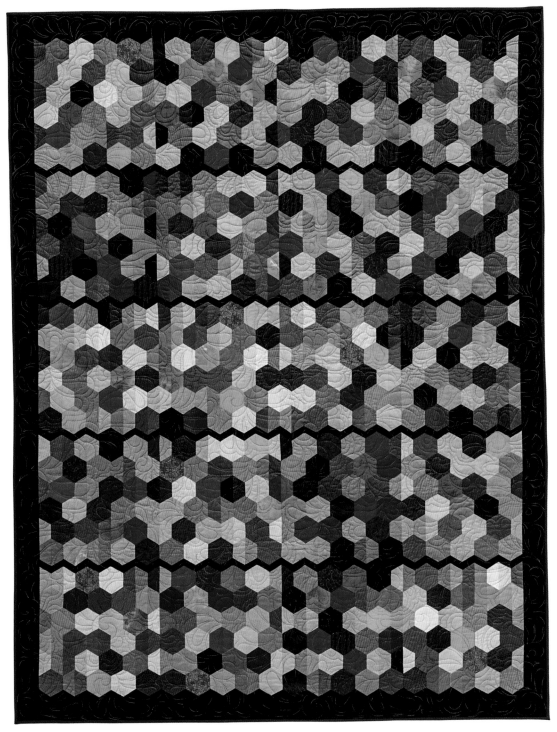

Made by Sara Nephew, quilted by Judy Irish

▲ **Finished block:** 12½" × 13¾"   ▲ **Finished quilt:** 55" × 73¾"

Sara used a random approach to choosing the colors and the light and dark values for this quilt—just having fun playing with all the solids. As a result, a careful examination of the quilt reveals the edges where the blocks meet. But that's okay—it's all part of the quilt design, including the black edge pieces that make a zigzag line that looks like rickrack at the top and bottom of each block!

YARDAGE

Light, medium, and dark gumballs: ¼ yard of 18–20 fabrics **or** ⅜ yard of 12–15 fabrics

Edge pieces (black): ⅔ yard

Border: ¾ yard

Binding: ⅝ yard

Backing: 4⅝ yards

Batting: 63″ × 82″

CUTTING

Gumball fabrics

- Cut 86 strips 1¾″ × width of fabric.

  Subcut 1,200 half-hexagons using the 3¼″ line on the ruler, following the directions in Cut Half-Hexagons (page 70).

Cut from 1¾″ with 3¼″ line.

Edge fabric

- Cut 13 strips 1½″ × width of fabric.

  Subcut 200 rectangles 1½″ × 2½″. Cut the rectangles into 200 left and 200 right triangle halves, following the instructions in Cut Triangle Halves (page 23).

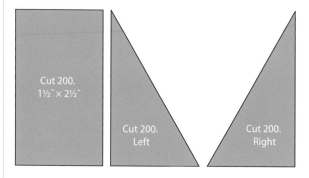

Borders

- Cut 7 strips 3″ × width of fabric.

Binding

- Calculate the size needed for your style of binding (see Figure *Your* Binding Width, page 21). Cut 7 width-of-fabric strips in that size.

CONSTRUCTION

Seam allowances are ¼" unless otherwise noted.

Piece the Blocks

Follow the arrows for pressing direction.

1. Arrange 60 half-hexagons in a 10 × 6 array and add the triangle halves to the top and bottom of the rows to make a block. (Note that half-hexagons match to create the look of a full hexagon.) When you are pleased with the arrangement, sew the pieces into columns, and then sew the columns together to make the block.

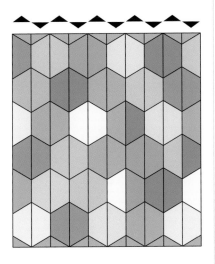

2. Repeat Step 1 to make 20 blocks. (Note that the half-hexagons at the edges do not have to match, but if you prefer, you can select the edge half-hexagons to complete the adjacent half-hexagon. Label the blocks to keep them in order.)

Piece the Quilt

1. Arrange the blocks as desired. Note that in order for the rickrack design to appear, the same edge of each block needs to be placed pointing up.

2. Sew the blocks into rows, and then sew the rows together to finish the quilt top.

3. Add the borders.

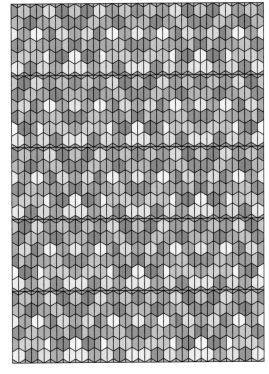

Piecing

Finish the Quilt

Layer, quilt, and bind to complete your quilt. Here is one suggestion for quilting that avoids the seam intersections.

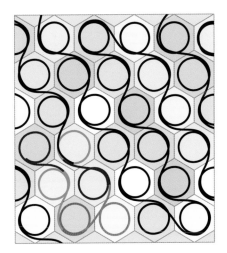

Detail of quilting

Gumball Variation *by Deborah Haynes*
Photo by Randy Pfizenmaier

Using flannel and larger pieces, Deb created a wonderfully cozy lap quilt. Using ½ yard each of 10–11 fabrics, she cut 3¼" strips into 6¼" half-hexagons. For the edges, she cut 2¼" × 4" rectangles to make triangle halves. All these pieces came together for a fast, fun quilt.

In this child's quilt, bright cheerful colors are front and center. With only 9 larger blocks, fewer pieces, and staggered half-hexagons, this design adds a lot of interest to the quilt. Add fun conversational prints for an I Spy game. Take 32 precut 2½"-wide strips and create stacks of 6 fabrics for quick cutting of 4¾" half-hexagons. Triangle halves are cut from 1⅞" × 3¼" rectangles. You will have the quilt made in no time!

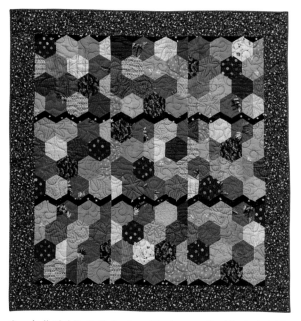

Gumball Child's Quilt *by Sara Nephew, quilted by Judy Irish*

Bubbles

Made by Diane Riley Coombs, quilted by Adrienne Reynolds

Photo by Randy Pfizenmaier

▲ **Finished quilt:** 59½˝ × 77½˝

To make this quilt, Diane chose the fabric and cut the pieces. Then Diane, Sara, and Sara's granddaughter Skye arranged and rearranged them until they liked the design. While Diane sat at the sewing machine and Sara made adjustments to the fabric positions, Skye picked up and carried the pieces to Diane. A lot of fun was had by all, as "many hands make light work."

YARDAGE

Light to dark bubbles: ⅛ yard of 45–48 fabrics, **or** ¼ yard of 23–26 fabrics, **or** 23–26 fat quarters

Edge pieces (print on white): ⅝ yard

Border: ⅝ yard

Binding: ¾ yard

Backing: 4¾ yards

Batting: 67" × 85"

CUTTING

Bubbles

- Cut 45 strips 4" × width of fabric from the light to dark fabrics.

  Subcut an even number of 7¾" half-hexagons from each fabric, for a total of at least 180. (Refer to Cut Half-Hexagons, page 70, as needed.)

Edge fabric

- Cut 3 strips 4" × width of fabric. Cut 12 half-hexagons.

- Cut 2 strips 2¾" × width of fabric.

  Subcut 16 rectangles 2¾" × 4¾". Cut 16 left and 16 right triangle halves, following the instructions in Cut Triangle Halves (page 23).

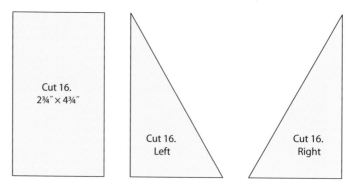

Borders

- Cut 7 strips 2¼" × width of fabric.

Binding

- Calculate the size needed for your style of binding (see Figure *Your* Binding Width, page 21). Cut 8 width-of-fabric strips in that size.

CONSTRUCTION

Seam allowances are ¼″ unless otherwise noted.

Piece the Quilt

Press the seams in each column in opposite directions. Before sewing and pressing, see Tip: Easy Directional Pressing (at right) for a method of staying organized when alternating pressing directions for each row.

1. Arrange the half-hexagons into a pleasing design. Add the edge pieces at the sides, top, and bottom

2. Sew the half-hexagons into columns. Join the columns together in pairs.

3. Sew pairs together, and then sew the remaining 3 seams. (I have found this method of pairing strips keeps an even piecing style throughout the quilt.)

Piecing

4. Add the borders.

tip

EASY DIRECTIONAL PRESSING — by Marci

When working on a project that indicated alternating rows should be pressed in opposite directions, I used to find myself frustrated (and with a headache). I finally realized it is best to do all the piecing first, followed by all the pressing. Here is how I press now:

1. *When it is time to press, pick up every other row, starting from the top, to create a stack.*

2. *Pick up every other row, starting from the bottom, to create a stack.*

3. *If the row is pressed toward the top, hold the top with the hand not holding the iron and press the seams toward that hand. Press all these rows first.*

4. *If the row is pressed toward the bottom, hold the bottom with the hand not holding the iron and press the seams toward that hand.*

Finish the Quilt

Layer, quilt, and bind to complete your quilt. Here is one suggestion for quilting.

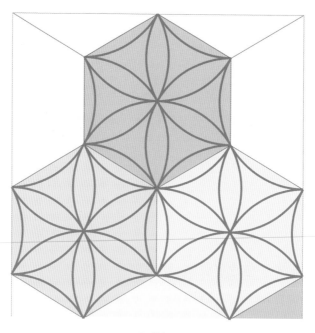

Quilting

 **VARIATIONS**

My Niece's Flower Garden *by Janice Schlieker, quilted by Marci Baker*

Starting with the bubbly center fabric, Janice found flowers emerging from this random hexagonal design, and they just kept on growing. It's made with clear, bright colors, with a solid and a print for each flower. Can't you see it on a teenage girl's bed? An easy way to have a long-lasting garden, this quilt is both refreshing and beautiful. Use 2½" strips, and cut half-hexagons with the 4¾" ruler line. Piece the half-hexagons in horizontal rows.

Reflections

Made by Jeanne Rumans

▲ **Finished block:** 12½″ × 13¾″   ▲ **Finished quilt:** 64″ × 82¾″

YARDAGE

Light to dark gradation:

A—Light 1 (light yellow): ⅞ yard

B—Light 2 (medium yellow): 1 yard

C—Medium 1 (brick orange with black/red): 1⅛ yards

D—Medium 2 (brick orange with black/gold): 1⅝ yards (includes Border 4)

E—Medium-dark 1 (fuchsia with black): ⅞ yard

F—Medium-dark 2 (mottled fuchsia): 1⅝ yards (includes Border 3)

G—Dark 1 (purple): 1¼ yards (includes Border 2)

H—Dark 2 (brick red): 1⅛ yard

Accent (blue-violet): 1⅛ yards (includes Border 1)

Binding: ¾ yard

Backing: 5⅛ yards

Batting: 72″ × 91″

---

tip

SWATCH CARD

To stay organized despite the large variety of fabrics, make some swatch cards. One card has all the fabrics placed in value order, and the second shows the placement of the fabrics across the block. Marci created these samples to illustrate the idea. They are not an exact match to Jeanne's quilt.

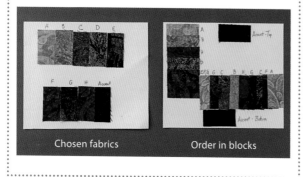

| Chosen fabrics | Order in blocks |

CUTTING

Gradation

- See the table below for the number of strips and the sizes to cut for *each* fabric. Then, following the instructions in Fast Cut Half-Hexagons (page 77), from 4¾″ strips, cut 1¾″ slices; then subcut the number of half-hexagons listed below, using the 3¼″ ruler line. Set the 3″-wide strips aside for the speed-pieced half-hexagons.

Fabric	Cut strips.	
	3″ × width of fabric	4¾″ × width of fabric
A	8	2; subcut into 60 half-hexagons
B	8	1; subcut into 20 half-hexagons
C	10	1; subcut into 20 half-hexagons
D	6	2; subcut into 60 half-hexagons
E	6	1; subcut into 20 half-hexagons
F	8	2; subcut into 40 half-hexagons
G	10	1; subcut into 20 half-hexagons
H	8	2; subcut into 40 half-hexagons

Accent

- Cut 13 strips 1½″ × width of fabric. Subcut into 200 rectangles 1½″ × 2½″.

  From the rectangles, cut 200 left and 200 right triangle halves, following the instructions in Cut Triangle Halves (page 23).

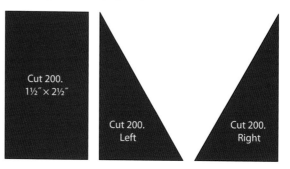

Cut 200. 1½″ × 2½″

Cut 200. Left

Cut 200. Right

Borders

- *Border 1:* Cut 7 strips 2″ × width of fabric from the accent fabric.

- *Border 2:* Cut 7 strips 2″ × width of fabric from fabric G.

- *Border 3:* Cut 7 strips 2″ × width of fabric from fabric F.

- *Border 4:* Cut 8 strips 3″ × width of fabric from fabric D.

Binding

- Calculate the size needed for your style of binding (see Figure *Your* Binding Width, page 21). Cut 8 width-of-fabric strips in that size.

CONSTRUCTION

Seam allowances are ¼″ unless otherwise noted.

Piece the Blocks

Follow the arrows for pressing direction. Follow the instructions in Speed Piece Half-Hexagons (page 71) as you piece the blocks.

1. Using the 3″ strips, sew the following pairs of strips together:

		B–H	G–E	D–A	F–C
Shifted left	**Sew pairs.**	4	3	3	5
	Pressing direction	Press to H.	Press to E.	Press to A.	Press to C.
Shifted right	**Sew pairs.**	4	3	3	5
	Pressing direction	Press to B.	Press to D.	Press to F.	Press to G.

2. Cut the following quantities of left and right hexalongs from the strip sets that have the 1¾″ slice size and the ruler line alignment for 3¼″.

	B–H	D–E	F–A	G–C
Cut hexalongs.	60 left, 60 right	40 left, 40 right	50 left, 50 right	80 left, 80 right

3. Arrange the pieces for one Reflection block and one Reverse Reflection block, following the diagrams below.

4. Sew the pieces into columns, pressing new seams in the opposite direction of the previous seams. Do not change the direction of the hexalong seams. Sew the strips together lengthwise in pairs and press to the right.

5. Sew pairs together and press to the right.

6. Repeat Steps 4–6 to make 10 Reflection blocks and 10 Reverse Reflection blocks.

Piece the Quilt

1. Arrange the blocks, alternating between Reflections blocks and Reverse Reflections blocks, to make rows of 4. Rotate the second and fourth rows of blocks 180°.

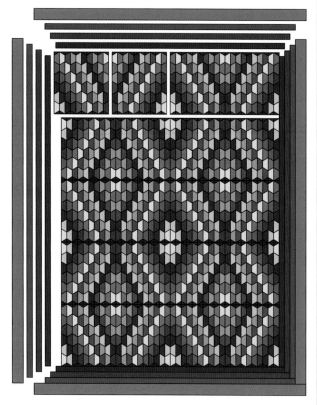

Piecing

2. Add the borders.

Finish the Quilt

Layer, quilt, and bind to complete your quilt. Here is one suggestion for quilting.

Quilting

Reflections Wallhanging *by Elaine Muzichuk, quilted by Sarah Beyer*

Four red-orange and five blue-green fabrics create a blazing quilt design. Using this complementary color combination, Elaine made the four blocks come together in the center for a focused design. With the added borders, Elaine continued the radiating effect. She used the same-size pieces as *Reflections*, with only one fourth the amount of fabric.

A splash of color, plus delicate floral prints, add to the appeal of this soft-looking quilt. The reversal of the pattern balances its strong design. The half-hexagons match more closely to look like complete hexagons—it's like seeing a garden in full bloom through a cut-glass window. Light, color, and sparkle combine in this visual experience.

Sara used 2½" strips, cut half-hexagons using the 4¾" ruler line, and made a total of 9 blocks for a quilt that can easily be made from a jelly roll or two. This resulted in a much larger finished project, great for a throw-size quilt.

Reflections Variation *by Sara Nephew, quilted by Judy Irish*

The Wave

Made by Deborah Haynes, quilted by Jeri Lindstrom

Photo by Randy Pfizenmaier

▲ **Finished quilt: 70˝ × 79½˝**

Shades of blue! It's fun and easy to look for different lights and darks of the same color and then put them all together. This sure looks like water! Add a few more rows and turn the quilt on its side—you'll see the waves marching toward you!

YARDAGE

Light to dark gradation:

A—Light 1: ⅞ yard

B—Light 2: ⅞ yard

C—Light-medium 1: ¾ yard

D—Light-medium 2: ¾ yard

E—Medium 1: ½ yard

F—Medium 2: ½ yard

G—Dark 1: ½ yard

H—Dark 2: ½ yard

Top and bottom fill (blue and white stripe): ⅜ yard

Border 1: ⅞ yard

Border 2: 1½ yards

Binding: ¾ yard

Backing: 5 yards

Batting: 78″ × 87″

CUTTING

Gradation

- Cut the number of 3¼″ strips and subcut the number of half-hexagons given in the table below, using the 6¼″ ruler line and following the instructions in Cut Half-Hexagons (page 70). Set aside the leftover pieces from the A and B strips.

	A	B	C	D	E	F	G	H
Cut 3¼″ strips.	6	6	6	6	3	3	4	4
Subcut half-hexagons.	35	35	35	35	14	14	21	21

Cut from 3¼″ with 6¼″ line.

- Cut strips of the fabrics listed in the table below into rectangles; then subcut into triangle halves, following the instructions in Cut Triangle Halves (page 23):

	A	B	E	F
Cut 3⅞″ strips.	1	1	1	1
Subcut 3⅞″ × 6¾″ rectangles.	2	2	4	4
Subcut triangle halves.	4 right	4 left	7 right	7 left

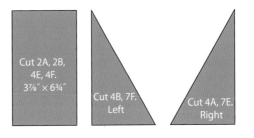

Cut 2A, 2B, 4E, 4F. 3⅞″ × 6¾″

Cut 4B, 7F. Left

Cut 4A, 7E. Right

Cutting list continues…

- Using the leftover 3¼" strips of fabrics A and B, cut 2 rectangles 2¼" × 4" from each fabric. Cut triangle halves from the rectangles: 4 right from A and 4 left from B. (There will be one extra of each.)

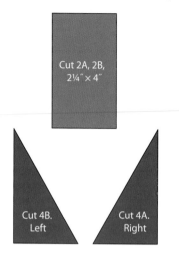

Cut 2A, 2B, 2¼" × 4"

Cut 4B. Left

Cut 4A. Right

Fill at top and bottom

- Cut 2 strips 3½" × width of fabric. Cut 30 triangles 3½" high, following the instructions in Cut Triangles (page 32).

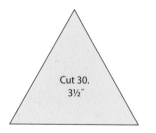

Cut 30. 3½"

Borders

- *Border 1:* Cut 7 strips 3½" × width of fabric.
- *Border 2:* Cut 7 strips 6½" × width of fabric.

Binding

- Calculate the size needed for your style of binding (see Figure Your Binding Width, page 21). Cut 9 width-of-fabric strips in that size.

CONSTRUCTION

Seam allowances are ¼" unless otherwise noted.

Piece the Rows

Follow the arrows for pressing direction.

This design is not sewn the way it is viewed, which is in vertical wavy lines. It is sewn instead in horizontal braid-like rows that build from the right side of the quilt. The braid starts with a base triangle and then is built with half-hexagons. Half of the braids start on the left side of the base triangle and the others start on the right side.

1. Make 3 stacks of half-hexagons for the left and 3 stacks for the right, according to the fabric order shown below for each braid.

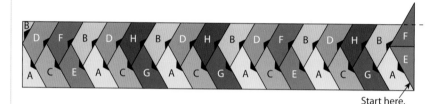

Start here.

Left braid: Make 3.

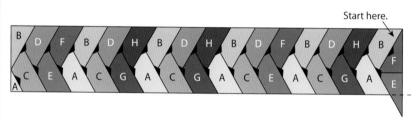

Start here.

Right braid: Make 3.

2. Piece 6 pairs of E and F triangle halves to make the braid bases. Using the stacks from Step 1, begin adding half-hexagons to the base on the appropriate side, left or right.

3. Add the next half-hexagon in the stack, matching at the top of the previous half-hexagon. Part of the base will be sticking out. This can be trimmed off after a few hexagons have been sewn onto the braid. Sew a total of 30 half-hexagons to each braid.

4. At the end of each braid, sew on 1 large triangle half and 1 small triangle half.

Make the Top and Bottom Rows

Starting with a large triangle half each for the top and bottom rows, add half-hexagons and triangles to complete the piecing of the rows in the order shown below.

Top row

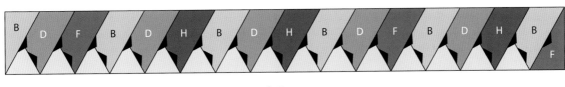

Bottom row

Piece the Quilt

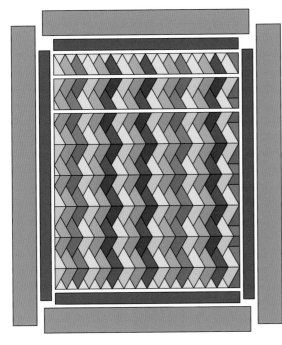

Piecing

1. Arrange the rows, alternating left and right rows, and then add the top and bottom rows. Sew the rows together to complete the quilt top.

2. Add the borders.

Finish the Quilt

Layer, quilt, and bind to complete your quilt. Here are several suggestions for quilting.

Quilting

Finished quilt: 60⅜" × 69¾"

Scott mixed an assortment of prints from a fabric line by Moda Fabrics, while keeping careful control of his color choices and the repetition within each wave. The results are inspiring!

The Wave I *by Scott Hansen, quilted by Becky Marshall*
Photo by Randy Pfizenmaier

Could Not Make Just One

Scott enjoyed the process of making the braids so much that he decided to make a second quilt from the same Moda fabric line. The name *The Wave* fits this colorway beautifully. Flexible fronds of kelp reach up through the water toward the sun. Little fish and snails are part of the ecosystem.

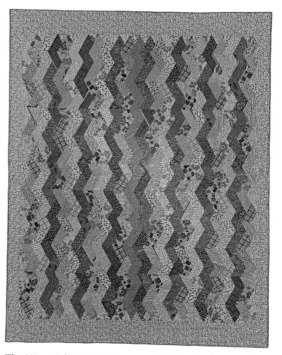

The Wave II *by Scott Hansen, quilted by Becky Marshall*
Photo by Randy Pfizenmaier

QUARTER-HEXAGONS

These instructions use the Clearview Triangle or Clearview Super 60 ruler (see Tools, page 14). If you choose to work with patterns instead, see Patterns (page 124).

Cut Quarter-Hexagons

There are several ways to cut these shapes. All of them start with a rectangle. Some rectangles, called singles, yield a single quarter-hexagon. These singles are great for charm quilts; for an example of a quilt that uses singles, see *Grand Hex* (page 94). Other rectangles, called doubles, yield two quarter-hexagons. There is a speed-piecing / cutting method for doubles that works wonderfully if there is repetition of fabric in the design.

This particular shape also is either a left or right. Keep this in mind when working through the projects and using these instructions. To cut both left and right pieces at the same time, stack the left fabric right side up and the right fabric wrong side up. Then cut either singles or doubles using the directions for left or right quarter-hexagons (at right).

SINGLES

1. Cut the appropriate size rectangle. (For this example we use a 2¾″ × 3¼″ rectangle.)

2. For left quarter-hexagons, position the rectangle horizontally, aligning the ruler so that the point is up and the center line is at the left edge of the fabric. Position the appropriate rule line for your project at the bottom of the rectangle (5¾″ in this example). Cut along the right side of the ruler.

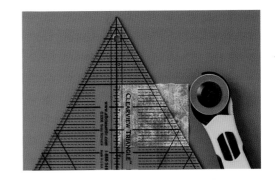

3. For right quarter-hexagons, position the rectangle horizontally, aligning the ruler so that the point is down and the center line is at the left edge of the fabric. Position the appropriate rule line for your project at the top of the rectangle (5¾″ in this example). Cut along the right side of the ruler.

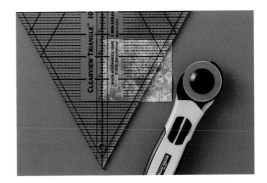

4. *Optional:* Trim the dog-ear off one corner to make the sewing easier and faster.

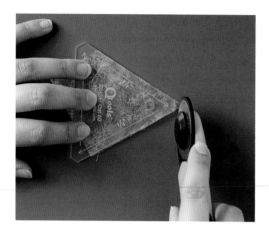

DOUBLES

1. Cut the appropriate size rectangle. (For this example we use a 2¾″ × 5″ rectangle.)

2. For left quarter-hexagons, position the rectangle horizontally, aligning the ruler so that the point is up and the center line is at the left edge of the fabric. Position the appropriate rule line for your project at the bottom of the rectangle (5¾″ in this example). The piece under the ruler should match the piece not under the ruler. Cut along the right side of the ruler.

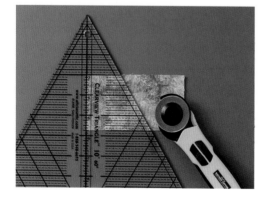

3. For right quarter-hexagons, position the rectangle horizontally, aligning the ruler so that the point is down and the center line is at the left edge of the fabric. Position the appropriate rule line for your project at the top of the rectangle (5¾″ in this example). The piece under the ruler should match the piece not under the ruler. If you find that one shape is consistently larger than the other, shift the ruler slightly so that the center line is on one side or the other of the left edge. (To mark this, see Tip: Never Forget the Cut Size, next page.) Cut along the right side of the ruler.

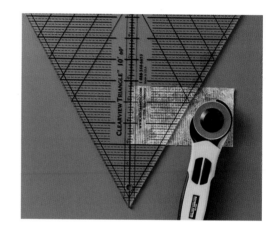

4. *Optional:* Trim the dog-ear off one corner to make the sewing easier and faster.

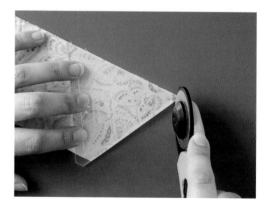

Speed Piece Quarter-Hexagons

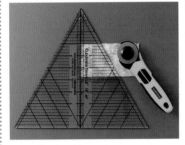
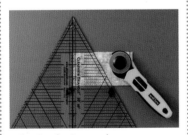
When there is repetition in the design, you can speed piece the quarter-hexagons by sewing doubles rectangles together and then cutting them. The process of sewing them into blocks changes, but it is well worth it, because the project can be made in less time.

Two Doubles

1. Cut the appropriate size rectangles. (For this example, we used 2¾″ × 5″.) Pair them as needed for the project, right sides together, and sew down both short sides of the rectangles.

2. Place the sewn rectangle horizontally, with the specified side up. Align the ruler so that the center line is at the left edge of the fabric and the designated rule line is at the bottom of the rectangle (5¾″ for this example). The piece under the ruler should match the piece not under the ruler. Cut along the right side of the ruler.

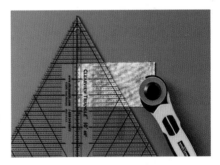

3. *Optional:* Before opening the unit, trim the dog-ears off one corner to make the sewing easier and faster.

Grand Hex

Made by Diane Riley Coombs, quilted by Becky Marshall

Photo by Randy Pfizenmaier

◀ **Finished block:** 26″ × 22½″   ◀ **Finished quilt:** 62″ × 77½″

Sky, sun, sand, water—what do you see in this fun quilt? Somehow the split triangle border becomes sunshine, and the blending and breaking of shapes becomes a moving world that is a real (and really happy) place.

YARDAGE

Charm quilt: 4¼″ × 5″ rectangles of 288 different fabrics

or

Variety, light to dark: 18 fat quarters **or** ⅜ yard of 15 fabrics

Border (red): 1¼ yard

Binding: ⅝ yard

Backing: 4⅞ yards

Batting: 70″ × 85″

CUTTING

Charm quilt

- Cut a quarter-hexagon from each 4¼″ × 5″ rectangle, using the 8¾″ rule line. (Refer to the Singles section in Cut Quarter-Hexagons, page 91, as needed.) Cut 144 left and 144 right quarter-hexagons. Set aside the leftover triangles for the border.

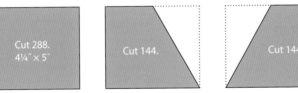

Left with 8¾″ line   *Right with 8¾″ line*

Variety quilt

- If using fat quarters, cut 4 strips from each fat quarter 4¼″ × 20″.

  From the strips, cut 144 rectangles, 4¼″ × 7⅝″.

- If using yardage, cut 2 strips from each fabric 4¼″ × width of fabric.

  From the strips, cut 144 rectangles, 4¼″ × 7⅝″.

- From the 144 rectangles, subcut 144 left and 144 right quarter-hexagons, using the 8¾″ rule line and the directions in the Doubles section of Cut Quarter-Hexagons (page 92).

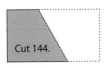

Left with 8¾″ line   *Right with 8¾″ line*

- For the border triangles, cut at least 74 rectangles 2½″ × 4¼″ and cut 74 left and 74 right triangle halves, following the directions in Cut Triangle Halves (page 23).

Border

- Cut 5 strips 3¾″ × width of fabric.

  Subcut into 70 triangles 3¾″ high.

  Subcut 4 corner squares 3½″ × 3½″.

- Cut 8 strips 2½″ × width of fabric.

  From 1 strip, cut 4 rectangles 2½″ × 4¼″. With 2 rectangles right side up and 2 right side down, cut on the diagonal to make 4 left and 4 right triangle halves.

  Set aside the other 7 strips for the outer border.

Binding

- Calculate the size needed for your style of binding (see Figure *Your* Binding Width, page 21). Cut 7 width-of-fabric strips in that size.

CONSTRUCTION

Seam allowances are ¼" unless otherwise noted.

Piece the Blocks

Follow the arrows for pressing direction.

Charm Quilt Planning

For her charm quilt, Diane had to plan the overall design of the quilt. Having a sketch or photo to refer to makes all the difference in the world. Use the block divisions to piece the quilt together in sections.

Variety Blocks

Arrange the left and right quarter-hexagons to make the 8 × 6 block. Place pieces randomly, or come up with your own unique design. Make 6 blocks.

Piece the Quilt

1. Arrange the 6 blocks and sew them together.

Piecing

2. To begin piecing the borders, select 148 of the triangles that were set aside. Sew into pairs to make 74 half-triangles.

Make 74 at 3¾" finished.

3. Arrange and piece the top and bottom borders, alternating half-triangles and cut border triangles. There are 16 pieced and 15 cut triangles in each border.

Make 2 with 16 pieced and 15 whole triangles.

4. Sew a 2½″ × 4¼″ triangle half to each end of the top and bottom borders. Pin the borders onto the quilt top. Adjust a few seams between triangles if needed to make the border match the quilt. Sew the borders to the quilt.

5. For the side borders, arrange 21 pieced and 20 cut triangles for each border. Sew triangles together, adding a 2½″ × 4¼″ triangle half to each end. Then sew a 3½″ × 3½″ corner square to each end.

Make 2 with 21 pieced and 20 whole triangles.

6. Pin the borders onto the quilt top. Adjust the border length as in Step 2, or remove a pieced triangle somewhere in the middle of the border so that a larger piece of border fabric can be added in. Can you see where that was done on this quilt? It is not easily seen, because the triangles blend in with the border randomly. Sew the borders to the quilt.

7. Add the outer borders.

Finish the Quilt

Layer, quilt, and bind to complete your quilt. Here are two suggestions for quilting: one for Diane's charm quilt and one for the variety design.

Quilting—Charm

Quilting—Variety

Piecing (with borders)

Pastels, checks, and big prints combine to create a comfy, restful quilt. It was so much fun to stack 4 layers of fabric to create new hexagon designs.

Here is how it was accomplished: Stack the 4 repeats of fabric and tack the layers together. Cut 5″ × 5″ squares. Arrange the squares so they match at the center point. Trim each square into a 4¼″ × 5″ rectangle.

Grand Hex with Repeats *by Sara Nephew, quilted by Judy Irish*

After you have completed cutting your rectangles, continue making the quilt according to the instructions for the main quilt.

Stacked Repeats Resources

For more information about stacked repeats, look for Sara Nephew's *Serendipity Quilts* and *Doubledipity*. (Both are available as eBooks from C&T Publishing.) We also recommend any one of Maxine Rosenthal's *One-Block Wonders*, *One-Block Wonders Encore!*, and *One-Block Wonders Cubed* (the latter two were co-written with Joy Pelzmann; all three are available from C&T Publishing).

Streaky

Made by Linda Tellesbo

Photo by Randy Pfizenmaier

◀ **Finished block:** 7″ × 12″   ◀ **Finished quilt:** 49″ × 60″

Diagonal strings of gems in rich colors make this deceptively simple quilt easy to enjoy in everyday living. The subtle mixing of red, green, and purple, contrasted with yellow, attracts the viewer's eye to the details. This pattern moves!

YARDAGE

Lights (yellows, tans): ¼ yard of 10 fabrics **or** 10 fat quarters

Darks (reds, greens): ¼ yard of 10 fabrics **or** 10 fat quarters

Binding: ½ yard

Backing: 3¼ yards

Batting: 57″ × 68″

CUTTING

Lights

- Cut a total of 32 strips 2¼″ × width of fabric. If using fat quarters, cut 64 strips 2¼″ × 20″.

  Subcut into 280 rectangles 2¼″ × 4⅛″. Cut 280 left and 280 right quarter-hexagons, using the 4¾″ ruler line and the instructions in Cut Quarter-Hexagons Doubles (page 92).

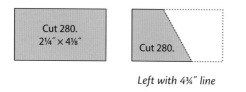

Left with 4¾″ line

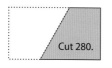

Right with 4¾″ line

Darks

- Cut a total of 32 strips 2¼″ × width of fabric. If using fat quarters, cut 64 strips 2¼″ × 20″.

  Subcut into 280 rectangles 2¼″ × 4⅛″. Cut 280 left and 280 right quarter-hexagons, using the 4¾″ ruler line and the instructions in Cut Quarter-Hexagons, Doubles (page 92).

Left with 4¾″ line

Right with 4¾″ line

Binding

- Calculate the size needed for your style of binding (see Figure *Your* Binding Width, page 21). Cut 6 width-of-fabric strips in that size.

CONSTRUCTION

Seam allowances are ¼" unless otherwise noted.

Piece the Blocks

Follow the arrows for pressing direction.

1. For each block select 16 light quarter-hexagons (8 left and 8 right) and 16 dark quarter-hexagons (8 left and 8 right). Piece them into 8 light/dark rectangles; press half of them with seams to the right and the other half with seams to the left. Piece 4 light/light rectangles , and 4 dark/dark rectangles and press the seams either way.

Make 8.

Make 4.

Make 4.

2. Piece 16 rectangles into a block, arranging so the seams follow the pressing directions.

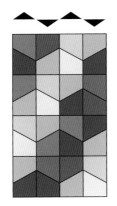

3. Repeat Steps 1 and 2 to make 35 blocks total. To piece all the rectangles first, make 280 light/dark rectangles, and 140 of each of the light/light and dark/dark rectangles.

Piece the Quilt

Piece the blocks into rows to complete the quilt top.

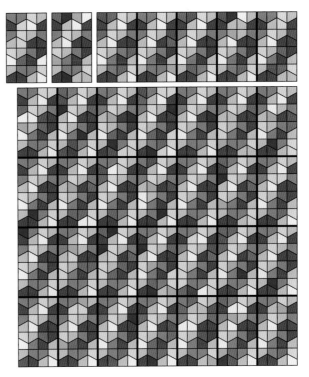

Piecing

Finish the Quilt

Layer, quilt, and bind to complete your quilt. Here are several suggestions for quilting that avoid the seam intersections.

Quilting

VARIATIONS

To figure yardage for adding blocks to Streaky, keep in mind that each 2¼" strip × width of fabric yields 9 rectangles. Each block needs 8 light rectangles and 8 dark rectangles. So for each additional block, add 1 strip 2¼" × width of fabric each of light and dark fabrics.

For a challenge, make a block and a reverse block and then arrange the blocks in a Trip Around the World style. To have a centered diamond, the layout needs to be evenly distributed in both directions, with a 6 × 6 grid being the closest to the project's layout as written.

This is a simple design—but one with a lot of possibilities. Gold, brown, green, and beige are easy and soothing to snuggle under. But what if each diagonal row was a different color? Or each bead on the string? Elaine used 2¾" × 5" rectangles, cutting them into quarter-hexagons with the 5¾" ruler line.

Streaky Quick Quilt *by Elaine Muzichuk, quilted by Sarah Beyer*

Photo by Randy Pfizenmaier

Watercolor Garden

Made by Sara Nephew, quilted by Pam J. Cope

◀ **Finished block:** 18″ × 17½″   ◀ **Finished quilt:** 63″ × 70″

Scraps of quilting fabric and decorator fabric combine in each block to suggest a sunshine-kissed, fragrant garden. It's helpful to use a design wall or flannel board to arrange a complete block and then simply sew up the rows and sew the rows together. This is a new approach to a popular traditional block.

YARDAGE

Medium to medium-dark flowers (Ring 1): ⅛ yard of 19 fabrics **or** 19 jelly roll strips

Light to light-medium flowers (Ring 2 and center): ⅛ yard of 41 fabrics **or** 41 jelly roll strips

Medium-dark to dark background: ⅛ yard of 35 fabrics **or** 35 jelly roll strips

Binding: ¾ yard

Backing: 4 yards

Batting: 71″ × 78″

---
note

If a less scrappy quilt is desired, use ¼ yard cuts. For Ring 1, gather 6 fabrics; for Ring 2 and center, use 15; and for background, use 11.

CUTTING

Flowers

- Cut the quantity of 2¼″ × width of fabric strips listed below for each design element. Subcut into 2¼″ × 4⅛″ rectangles as noted. Cut the number of background quarter-hexagons using the 4¾″ ruler line and following the instructions in Cut Quarter-Hexagons, Doubles (page 92).

	Ring 1	Ring 2 / center	Background
Cut 2¼″ strips.	19	41	35
Subcut 2¼″ × 4⅛″ rectangles.	168	364	308
Subcut quarter-hexagons.	—	—	140 left, 140 right

Binding

- Calculate the size needed for your style of binding (see Figure *Your* Binding Width, page 21). Cut 8 width-of-fabric strips in that size.

CONSTRUCTION

Seam allowances are ¼″ unless otherwise noted.

Piece the Blocks

Follow the arrows for pressing direction.

1. Make a variety of combinations by pairing rectangles, right sides together, within the same fabric type. For example, pair a Ring 1 fabric with another Ring 1 fabric, or a background rectangle with another background rectangle.) Do not mix fabrics types.

	Ring 1	Ring 2 / center	Background
Pairs of rectangles	84	182	84
Pairs of quarter-hexagons	168	364	168

2. Sew and cut quarter-hexagons, using the 4¾" rule line and following the instructions in Speed Piece Quarter-Hexagons (page 93). Because this design uses half-hexagons of a single value that have no left or right, the rectangle pairs can be cut either left or right.

3. Arrange 12 Ring 1, 26 Ring 2 and center, and 12 background quarter-hexagon pairs for a block. Fill the edges with 10 left and 10 right background quarter-hexagons. Finger-press lightly as you sew the blocks together. (It is not worth the headache to arrange the hexagons and press them fully, only to lay them out again.) Sew the quarter-hexagons into rows across the block, and then sew the rows together to finish a block.

4. Repeat Step 3 to make 12 blocks and 4 half-blocks.

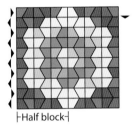

├ Half block ┤

Piece the Quilt

Arrange the blocks and half-blocks. Piece the blocks into rows across the quilt. Then sew the rows together. For assembling tips, see Tip: Easier Assembly (at right).

Piecing

Finish the Quilt

Layer, quilt, and bind to complete your quilt. Here is one suggestion for quilting that avoids the seam intersections.

Quilting for one block

---

tip

EASIER ASSEMBLY ○—[*by Sara*]

I glued batting to an 18" × 20" piece of foam core and used this board to arrange all the quarter-hexagon pairs in the proper order for sewing. (Flannel also works for this.) This keeps the block together while I work on it and makes assembling the pieces much easier.

Watercolor Garden Quick Quilt

Made by Sara Nephew, quilted by Marci Baker

◀ **Finished block:** 24″ × 22½″　　◀ **Finished quilt:** 62″ × 81½″

With its bright, cheery fabrics from Maywood Studio, this quilt is perfect for a young girl. The twin-size quilt features a 10" drop. Wider borders can be added if needed, and the quilt comes together quickly with strip piecing. Enjoy creating a garden in your corner of the world.

YARDAGE

Flowers: ⅓ yard of 10–12 fabrics **or** 10–12 fat quarters

Background: 1⅞ yards (includes border corners) of a medium-size print

Border: 1½ yards for crosswise cuts **or** 2 yards for lengthwise cuts

Binding: ¾ yard

Backing: 5¼ yards

Batting: 70" × 89"

CUTTING

Flowers

- From each fabric cut 3 strips 2¾" × width of fabric. Subcut into 24 rectangles 2¾" × 5" for at least 228 rectangles.

> ### note
>
> *This project is a good candidate for using Sara's design board organizational technique (see Tip: Easier Assembly, page 105).*

Background

- Cut 17 strips 2¾" × width of fabric.

  Subcut into 132 rectangles 2¾" × 5". Cut 60 left and 60 right quarter-hexagons, using the 5¾" ruler line and following the instructions in Cut Quarter-Hexagons, Doubles (page 92).

- Cut 1 strip 7½" × width of fabric. Subcut 4 squares 7½" × 7½". Save these for the border.

Borders

- Cut 6 strips 7½" × width of fabric.

Binding

- Calculate the size needed for your style of binding (see Figure *Your* Binding Width, page 21). Cut 8 width-of-fabric strips in that size.

CONSTRUCTION

Seam allowances are ¼" unless otherwise noted.

Piece the Blocks

Follow the arrows for pressing direction.

Notice in Sara's quilt how some of the hexagons have a high contrast, like the pink flowers, while others blend in and look almost like full hexagons, like the pink-and-orange flower.

1. Pair the fabrics you have chosen for 1 flower block. Each hexagon in the design comprises 2 rectangles sewn together.

- For the center of each flower, pair 2 rectangles.

- For Ring 1 of each flower, pair 12 rectangles.

- For Ring 2 of each flower, pair 24 rectangles.

- For a hexagon that is all one fabric, pair 2 rectangles of the same fabric together.

- For a checkerboard effect, pair rectangles of the same two fabrics.

- For the background, pair 12 rectangles of the background fabric.

Sometimes I am asked why I cut 2 pieces of fabric just to sew them back together. The smaller pieces fit better than using larger pieces, and rearranging a printed fabric with piecing adds a completely new texture.

2. Sew the paired rectangles together down both short sides.

3. Cut, using the 5¾" ruler line and following the instructions in Speed Piece Quarter-Hexagons (page 93). For the checkerboard effect around the entire flower, cut 4 left and 2 right for Ring 1, and 8 left and 4 right for Ring 2. Make a total of 228 flower quarter-hexagon pairs and 72 background quarter-hexagon pairs.

4. To make one block, arrange 38 flower and 12 background quarter-hexagon pairs. Fill the edges with 10 left and 10 right background quarter-hexagons. Sew the quarter-hexagons into rows across the block. If needed, change direction of previously pressed seams. Then sew the rows together to finish a block.

5. Repeat Step 4 to make 4 blocks and 4 half-blocks.

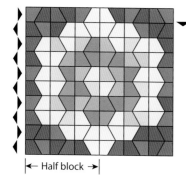

|← Half block →|

Piece the Quilt

1. Arrange the blocks and half-blocks. Piece the blocks into rows across the quilt. Then sew the rows together.

Piecing

2. Measure and cut side, top, and bottom borders. Sew on top and bottom borders.

3. Join the squares of background fabric to the ends of the side borders. Sew on the side borders.

Finish the Quilt

Layer, quilt, and bind to complete your quilt. Here is one suggestion for quilting that avoids the seam intersections.

This quilting design shows pebbles surrounding the flower. Notice the different sizes at each corner. The larger pebbles are too close in size to the outer petals. This makes it hard to distinguish the flower from the background. The next two pebble sizes better show off the flower. The smallest pebble size may look nice, but it takes longer to do, and it lends a stiffness to the quilt that can cause distortion.

Quilting

VARIATIONS

The following three quilts use a version of the Watercolor block with only one ring of color for the flower. Notice how value and color play with the overall effect of each quilt. To replicate one of these quilts, use the sizes listed in each description and the basic block layout as your guide.

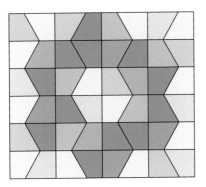

Mom's Flower *by Sara Nephew, quilted by Judy Irish*

The patterns made from quarter-hexagons look so much like traditional hexagon patterns that it's tempting to make them in traditional colors, such as 1930s fabrics and pastels. This is one of Sara's interpretations of that classic look, using today's fabrics. This project uses 2¼″ × 4⅛″ rectangles and the 4¾″ ruler line to cut quarter-hexagons.

Variations continues…

VARIATIONS

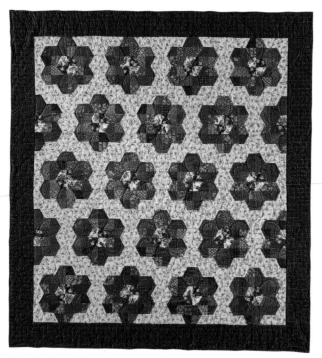

Red and white is a favorite color choice for quilts. Annette mixed a variety of red prints with a simpler background fabric. She split the center of the flower to add a checkerboard triangle to the design. This is such a lovely quilt, just begging to be wrapped around someone—and *that special someone* will know Mom loves them. This project uses 2¼″ × 4⅛″ rectangles and the 4¾″ ruler line to cut quarter-hexagons.

Mom's Flower Variation by Annette Austin, quilted by Becky Marshall
Photo by Randy Pfizenmaier

Somehow the mix of dark- and light-colored fabrics with warm- and cool-colored fabrics pulls together the little posies in this quilt. Then all the colors become the border, too. (You'll notice the border is cleverly made from extra rectangles.) Fun to look at and fun to make! Janet used larger flannel pieces for her variation—2¾″ × 5″ rectangles and the 5¾″ ruler line to cut quarter-hexagons.

Mom's Flower Variation by Janet Blazekovich
Photo by Randy Pfizenmaier

Diamond Path

Made by Joyce Lawrence Cambron

Photo by Randy Pfizenmaier

◀ **Finished block:** 16½″ × 28½″   ◀ **Finished quilt:** 62½″ × 84¼″

Hot and cold colors play off one another, adding motion to what could otherwise be a static design. Do you see orange diamonds or blue diamonds? Add to this a variety of prints and values and your eye moves across the scene.

How Fabrics Play Together
○— **by Marci**

Early on in my quilting life, I found selecting more than 6 or 7 fabrics for a quilt to be daunting. But one of my early teachers explained that those are actually the hardest quilts to make successfully, because if one fabric is not a great selection, it will stand out like a sore thumb. When you select a lot of fabrics in the same range, one is less likely to stand out, because there is less of it—and chances are there is another fabric similar to it. I think of it as, "Everyone can find a friend in a crowd, rather than standing out in the crowd and taking away from the whole."

If you struggle with choosing fabrics, try replacing one fabric with 5 fabrics or more. My early quilts would have 30–35 fabrics. Building a stash is the first step. With all the precuts available today, building up your stash is easier than ever. Sara finds a lot of fabrics at garage sales. I have gathered from my grandmother's and mother's fabric collections. Another option to expand your collection is to swap extra fabric with friends or with quilting guild members. Look online for a fabric trading club. And don't worry that you might get an ugly fabric—even ugly fabrics can blend in and add interest and depth to the project!

YARDAGE

Diamond 1 (blue): ⅛ yard of 23–25 fabrics **or** ¼ yard of 12–14 fabrics

Diamond 2 (orange): ⅛ yard of 23–25 fabrics **or** ¼ yard of 12–14 fabrics

Border 1: ½ yard

Border 2: 1⅜ yards

Binding: ¾ yard

Backing: 5⅛ yards

Batting: 70″ × 92″

CUTTING

Diamonds

- Cut the quantity of 3¼″ × width of fabric strips listed for Diamond 1 and Diamond 2 below. Subcut into 3¼″ × 5⅞″ rectangles. From a few of the rectangles, cut the number of quarter-hexagons, using the 6¾″ ruler line and following the instructions in Cut Quarter-Hexagons, Doubles (page 92).

	Diamond 1 (blue)	Diamond 2 (orange)
Cut 3¼″ strips.	23	23
Subcut 3¼″ × 5⅞″ rectangles.	135	135
Subcut quarter-hexagons.	15 left, 15 right	33 left, 33 right

Borders

- *Border 1:* Cut 7 strips 1½″ × width of fabric.
- *Border 2:* Cut 7 strips 6″ × width of fabric.

Binding

- Calculate the size needed for your style of binding (see Figure *Your* Binding Width, page 21). Cut 8 width-of-fabric strips in that size.

CONSTRUCTION

Seam allowances are ¼″ unless otherwise noted.

Piece the Blocks

Follow the arrows for pressing direction.

1. Pair rectangles, right sides together, within the same hue. For example, pair a Diamond 1 fabric with another Diamond 1 fabric. Do not mix hues.

	Diamond 1 (blue)	Diamond 2 (orange)
Pairs of rectangles	60	51
Pairs of quarter-hexagons	120	102

2. Sew and cut quarter-hexagons, using 6¾″ rule line and following the instructions in Speed Piece Quarter-Hexagons (page 93). Because this design uses single-value half-hexagons that have no left or right, the rectangle pairs may be cut either left or right.

3. Arrange 16 Diamond 1 quarter-hexagon pairs and 14 Diamond 2 quarter-hexagon pairs into the center portion of the block. Fill the edges with 4 Diamond 1 quarter-hexagon pieces (2 left and 2 right), and 8 Diamond 2 quarter-hexagon pieces (4 left and 4 right). Sew the pieces into columns down the block. Then sew the columns together to finish the block.

4. Repeat Step 3 to make 6 blocks and 3 half-blocks, using 6 quarter-hexagon pieces for the Diamond 2 centers for the half-blocks.

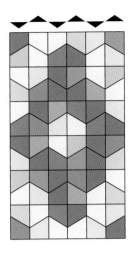

Piece the Quilt

1. Arrange the blocks and half-blocks. Piece the blocks into rows across the quilt. Then sew the rows together.

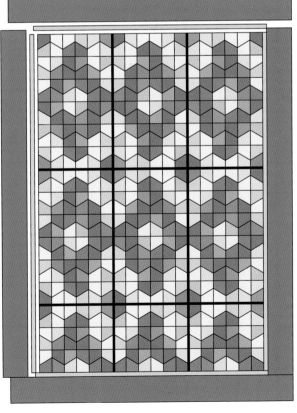

Piecing

2. Add the borders.

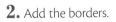

Finish the Quilt

Layer, quilt, and bind to complete your quilt. Here is one suggestion for quilting that includes a partial motif for the half-blocks.

Quilting

 **VARIATIONS**

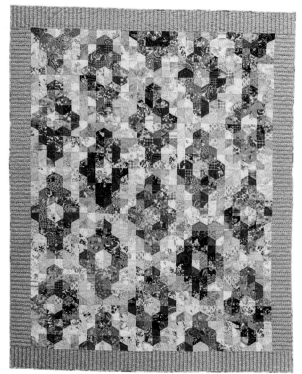

Use your scraps to make a light and lively quilt. Green, red, and blue mix with the light yellow-gold background fabric to make a cozy, friendly quilt that anyone will love. Sunshine strikes through the diamond garden path.

Diamond Path Variation *by Sara Nephew*

Sparkling Diamond

Made by Jeanne Rumans

Photo by Randy Pfizenmaier

◀ **Finished block:** 24½″ × 30″   ◀ **Finished quilt:** 60″ × 71″

In this quilt Jeanne made the diamonds sparkle by using strong contrast and bright, cool colors. She controlled the placement of light and dark values to create a strong overall design.

YARDAGE

Light diamonds:

⅛ yard of at least 31 fabrics

or ⅓ yard of at least 11 fabrics

Medium diamonds:

⅛ yard of at least 18 fabrics

or ⅓ yard of at least 6 fabrics

Dark diamonds:

⅛ yard of at least 15 fabrics

or ⅓ yard of at least 5 fabrics

Border 1: ⅜ yard

Border 2: ⅜ yard

Border 3: 1⅛ yards

Binding: ¾ yard

Backing: 3⅞ yards

Batting: 68″ × 79″

CUTTING

Diamonds

- Cut the quantity of 2¼″ × width of fabric strips listed for each fabric range below. Subcut the 2¼″ × 4⅛″ rectangles. Cut the number of quarter-hexagons given, using the 4¾″ ruler line and following the instructions in Cut Quarter-Hexagons, Doubles (page 92).

	Light	Medium	Dark
Cut 2¼″ strips.	31	18	15
Subcut 2¼″ × 4⅛″ rectangles.	272	160	128
Subcut quarter-hexagons.	48 left, 48 right	32 left, 32 right	32 left, 32 right

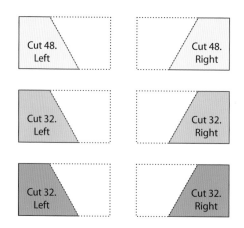

Borders

- *Border 1:* Cut 6 strips 1½″ × width of fabric.

- *Border 2:* Cut 6 strips 1½″ × width of fabric.

- *Border 3:* Cut 7 strips 4″ × width of fabric.

Binding

- Calculate the size needed for your style of binding (see Figure *Your* Binding Width, page 21). Cut 8 width-of-fabric strips in that size.

CONSTRUCTION

Seam allowances are ¼" unless otherwise noted.

Piece the Blocks

Follow the arrows for pressing direction.

The block is pieced in quarters, with 2 sub-blocks and 2 reverse sub-blocks.

1. Sew and cut quarter-hexagon pairs from the rectangles in the quantities listed in the table below, using the 4¾" ruler line and following the instructions in Speed Piece Quarter-Hexagons (page 93). Because this design uses single-value half-hexagons that have no left or right, the rectangle pairs may be cut either left or right.

	Light	Medium	Dark
Pairs of rectangles	112	64	48
Pairs of quarter-hexagons	224	128	96

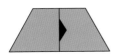

Make 224 with 4¾" ruler line.

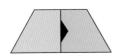

Make 128 with 4¾" ruler line.

Make 96 with 4¾" ruler line.

2. Arrange 6 dark quarter-hexagon pairs, 14 light quarter-hexagon pairs, and 8 medium quarter-hexagon pairs into the center portion of the block. Fill the edges with 4 dark (2 left and 2 right), 6 light (3 left and 3 right), and 4 medium (2 left and 2 right) quarter-hexagons. Sew the pieces into columns down the block. Then sew the columns together to finish the sub-block. Repeat this step to make 8 sub-blocks.

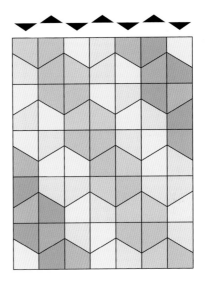

3. Repeat Step 2, using the same elements but in reverse. Make 8 reverse sub-blocks.

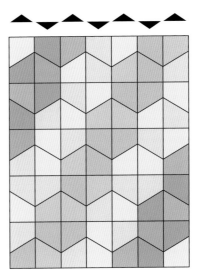

4. Using the sub-blocks and reverse sub-blocks, make 4 blocks.

Piece the Quilt

1. Arrange the blocks. Piece the blocks into rows across the quilt. Then sew the rows together.

Piecing

2. Add the borders.

Finish the Quilt

Layer, quilt, and bind to complete your quilt. Here is one suggestion for quilting each diamond.

Quilting

Jeanne did this second quilt in a different, watercolor-like colorway. In lilac the colors feel like blossoms. They are so floral and soft that you can almost smell them.

Sparkling Diamond *by Jeanne Rumans*
Photo *by Randy Pfizenmaier*

After seeing other fabrics in this traditional hexagon layout, Sara needed to see this quilt in 1930s-inspired colors and patterns; she even used some vintage fabrics from that decade. The result is a glowing quilt with lots of strong color and contrasts. Definitely abstract art!

Notice how Sara arranged the 4 sub-blocks into a diamond. The benefit to this arrangement is that when the corners come together in the middle, a fifth diamond is created.

Sparkling Diamond *by Sara Nephew*

Fancy Flowers

Made by Pam J. Cope and Sara Nephew, quilted by Jeanne Rumans

◀ **Finished block:** 14″ × 18″   ◀ **Finished quilt:** 65″ × 81″

Pam and Sara each made blocks for this quilt. Pam used mostly 1930s reprints for a light floral look, while Sara added some stronger 1930s colors. The mix is interesting and effective. This color variation of the Fancy pattern looks like rows of flowers growing in a garden behind the white picket fence. A narrow border of 30s green and a sprightly blue print are the perfect finish.

YARDAGE

Flowers (various colors): ⅛ yard of 8 or 9 fabrics each of 5 or 6 colorways (43 fabrics total)

Centers (yellow): ⅛ yard of 8 fabrics

Leaves (green): ⅛ yard of 22 fabrics

Picket fence (white prints): ⅛ yard of 15 fabrics

Border 1: ½ yard

Border 2: 1⅛ yards

Binding: ¾ yard

Backing: 5 yards

Batting: 73″ × 89″

CUTTING

Flowers, centers, and leaves

- Cut the quantity of 2¼″ strips × width of fabric strips listed below for each fabric. Subcut 2¼″ × 4⅛″ rectangles. Cut the number of quarter-hexagons, using the 4¾″ ruler line and following the instructions in Cut Quarter-Hexagons, Doubles (page 92).

	Flowers (per 5 or 6 colorways)	Center	Leaves	Picket fence
Cut 2¼″ strips.	8 or 9 (43 total)	8	22	15
Subcut 2¼″ × 4⅛″ rectangles.	24 per block for 16 blocks (384 total)	64	192	128
Subcut quarter-hexagons.	—	—	—	128 left, 128 right

Cut 128. Left   Cut 128. Right

Borders

- *Border 1:* Cut 7 strips 1½″ × width of fabric.

- *Border 2:* Cut 8 strips 4″ × width of fabric.

Binding

- Calculate the size needed for your style of binding (see Figure *Your* Binding Width, page 21). Cut 8 width-of-fabric strips in that size.

CONSTRUCTION

Seam allowances are ¼" unless otherwise noted.

Piece the Blocks

Follow the arrows for pressing direction.

1. Make a variety of combinations by pairing rectangles, right sides together, as listed below.

	Flowers (per 5 colorways)	Center	Leaves
Pairs of rectangles	32–39 per colorway (192 minimum)	32	96
Pairs of quarter-hexagons	64–77 per colorway (384 minimum)	64	192

2. Sew and cut quarter-hexagon pairs from the rectangles, using the 4¾" ruler line and following the instructions in Speed Piece Quarter-Hexagons (page 93). Because this design uses single-value half-hexagons that have no left or right, the rectangle pairs may be cut either left or right.

Make 64–77 of 5 or 6 colorways with 4¾" ruler line.

Make 64 flower centers with 4¾" ruler line.

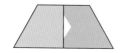

Make 192 leaves with 4¾" ruler line.

3. Arrange 4 center quarter-hexagon pairs, 12 quarter-hexagon pairs of one flower, 6 quarter-hexagon pairs each of two flowers, and 12 quarter-hexagon leaf pairs into the center of a block. Fill the edges with 16 picket fence quarter-hexagons (8 left and 8 right). Sew the pieces into columns down the block. Then sew the columns together to finish the block. Press the seams in each column in opposite directions. Repeat this step to make 16 blocks total, matching the half-flowers if desired. Pam and Sara had fun mixing their flowers so that they appeared to be overlapping.

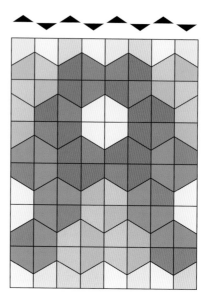

Piece the Quilt

1. Arrange the blocks. Piece the blocks into rows across the quilt. Then sew the rows together.

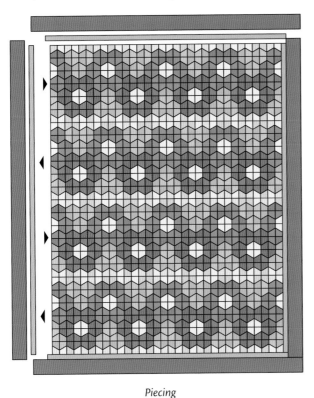

Piecing

2. Add the borders.

Finish the Quilt

Layer, quilt, and bind to complete your quilt. Here is one suggestion for quilting.

Quilting

VARIATIONS

The quarter-hexagon shape can make many designs, as seen in this variation of the Fancy Flower block. The value changes look like strips of lace added to a garment or put on the edge of a shelf or window. Try your own hand at a new creation. Make it fancy!

Fancy Lace *by Sara Nephew, quilted by Pam J. Cope*

Patterns

All patterns include seam allowances. These patterns can also be used to verify proper rotary cutting.

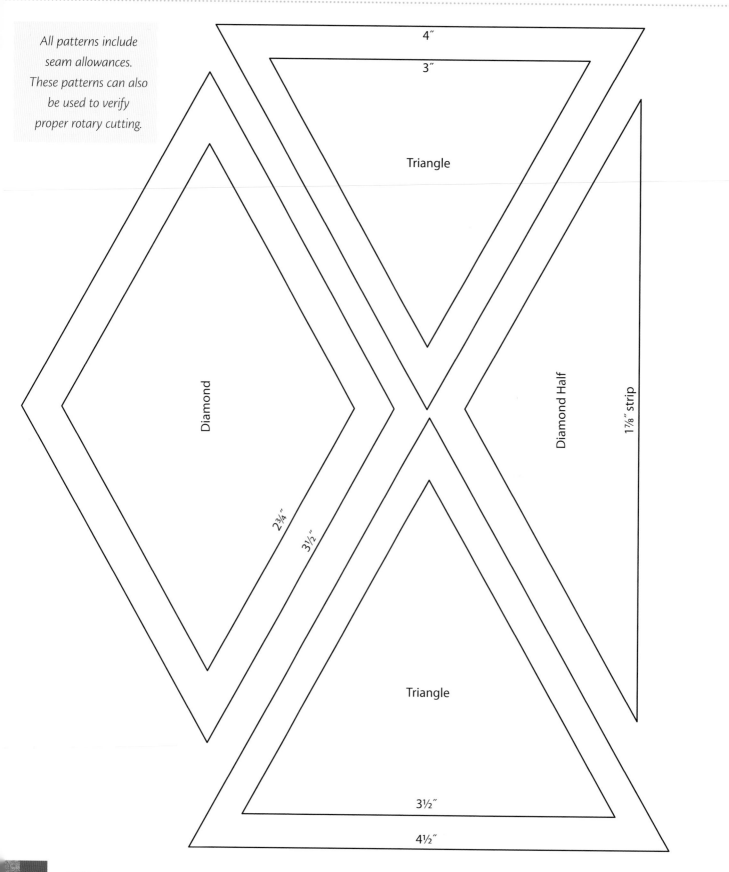

4″

3″

Triangle

Diamond

Diamond Half

1⅞″ strip

2¾″

3½″

Triangle

3½″

4½″

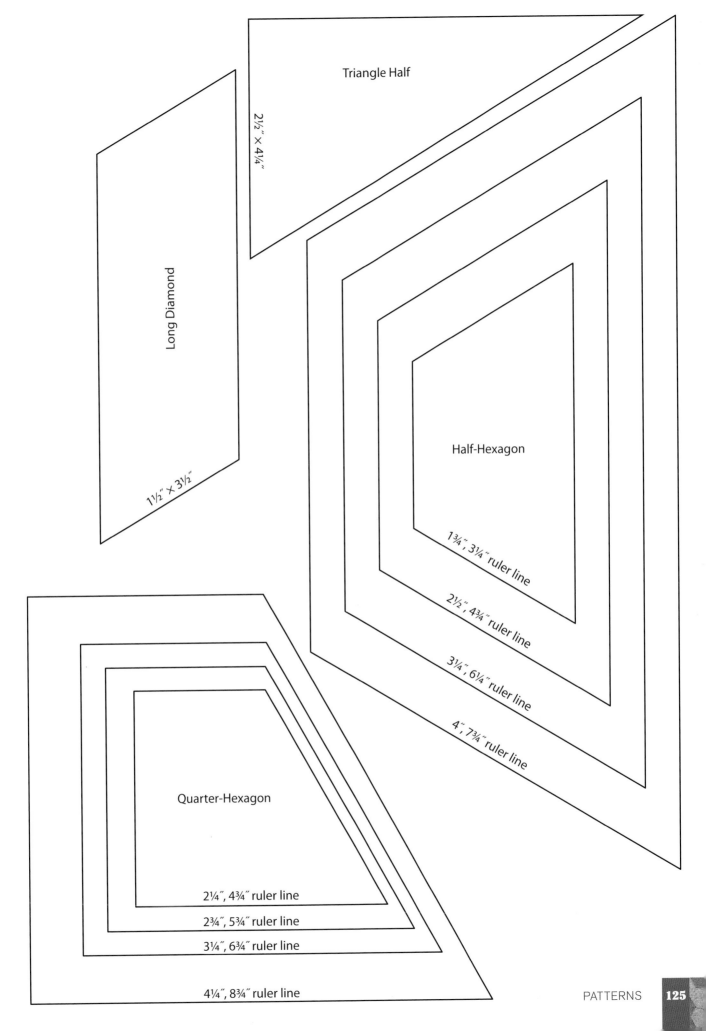

Triangle Half

2½" × 4¼"

Long Diamond

1½" × 3½"

Half-Hexagon

1¾", 3¼" ruler line

2½", 4¾" ruler line

3¼", 6¼" ruler line

4", 7¾" ruler line

Quarter-Hexagon

2¼", 4¾" ruler line

2¾", 5¾" ruler line

3¼", 6¾" ruler line

4¼", 8¾" ruler line

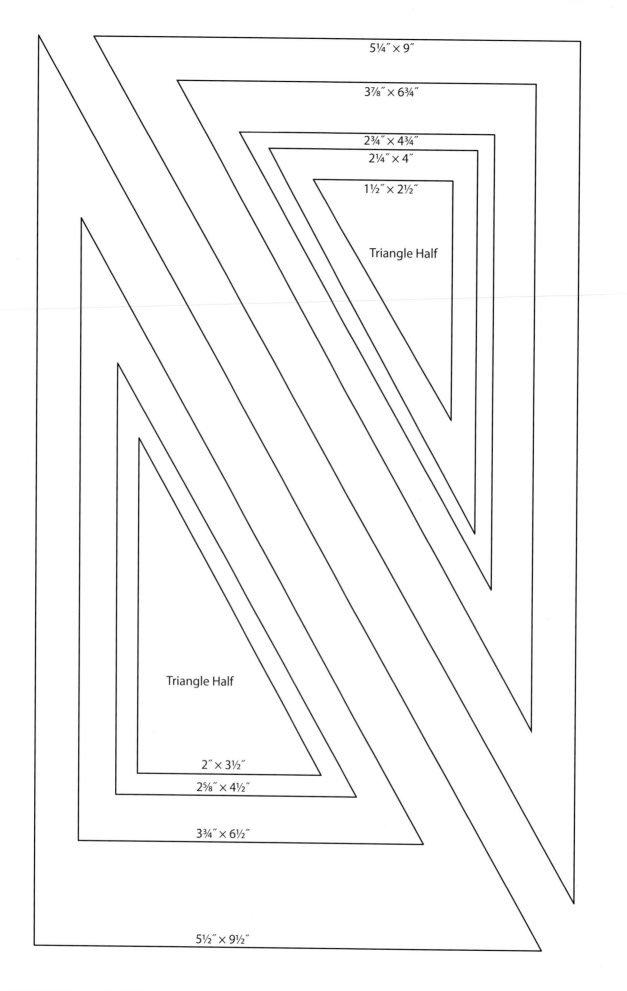

5¼″ × 9″

3⅞″ × 6¾″

2¾″ × 4¾″

2¼″ × 4″

1½″ × 2½″

Triangle Half

Triangle Half

2″ × 3½″

2⅝″ × 4½″

3¾″ × 6½″

5½″ × 9½″

About the Authors

Photo by Randy Pfizenmaier

Marci Baker

Recognized internationally for her expertise in quilting, Marci enjoys sharing ideas that simplify the quilting process. A native of Dallas, Texas, Marci began teaching quilting in 1989 for her local quilting guild and shops. In 1993 she started Alicia's Attic, a company that combines her love of math and teaching with her love of quilting.

As an admirer of traditional quilts, Marci was inspired to author the *Not Your Grandmother's Quilts* series, which uses traditional patterns that people associate with grandmothers but simplifying the techniques. In 2006 she expanded Alicia's Attic by purchasing Clearview Triangle from Sara Nephew. Marci and Sara are collaborating on new designs and techniques, with Marci traveling and teaching under her new business name: Quilt with Marci Baker. One of her latest adventures is the Quilt with Marci Baker Certification Program. With certified teachers across the United States and Canada, her methods are readily accessible through shops, guilds, and shows.

Marci and her husband, Clint, live in Fort Collins, Colorado, where they enjoy the beautiful mountain views.

Visit Marci's website, quiltwithmarcibaker.com, for her latest schedule. Contact her at marcibaker@quiltmb.com.

Photo by Rowland Studios

Sara Nephew

Sara is a quilt designer, author, and teacher who has developed several isometric (60°) triangle rulers. Sara's quilting career has taken her all over the United States, Canada, and Australia. Her quilts have been widely exhibited, and she has been featured in magazine articles and books.

Always an artist, Sara started her career as a commercial jeweler and began to learn diamond setting as well as continuing her work with painting and cloisonné enameling. After several other careers, Sara gravitated toward quilting and found her calling.

When Sara started the Clearview Triangle business, her multifaceted quilting career took off. In 2006 she retired from the day-to-day operations of running her business and sold her company to Marci Baker of Alicia's Attic. But Sara has not stopped working, creating new quilts, or writing, as evidenced by this book!

Contact Sara at saranephew@quiltmb.com.

Also by Marci Baker and Sara Nephew:

Also by Marci Baker:

Want even more creative content?

Make it, snap it, share it *using #ctpublishing*